AWAKEN AND JOURNEY TO YOUR TRUE SELF

Dr. Merlin Pickston

BALBOA.PRESS
A DIVISION OF HAY HOUSE

Balboa Press books may be ordered through booksellers or by contacting:

Balboa Press
A Division of Hay House
1663 Liberty Drive
Bloomington, IN 47403
www.balboapress.co.uk
UK TFN: 0800 0148647 (Toll Free inside the UK)
UK Local: 02036 956325 (+44 20 3695 6325 from outside the UK)

Print information available on the last page.

ISBN: 978-1-9822-8360-5 (sc)
ISBN: 978-1-9822-8362-9 (hc)
ISBN: 978-1-9822-8361-2 (e)

Balboa Press rev. date: 06/08/2021

CONTENTS

ACKNOWLEDGEMENTS

The birthing of this book has taken some time, the actual writing just about a year but the years of preparation, developing and using the tools I discuss in the book as a part of my own journey to my true self also contributed to the content, and took years.

I would like to thank my wife Lyz for providing me with endless opportunities for learning.

To the Trinity, our beautiful connection has helped so much in my journey and in the development of this book, the hours of conversation, advice, wisdom, support and unconditional love, thank you from the bottom of my heart.

A big thank you to Kaia Ra®, not only for bringing The Sophia Code® to earth at this time but for your steadfast strength and vulnerability in showing up in your HUGE leadership role. You inspire me every time I connect with you and I will be eternally grateful for the part the codex and you played in my continued journey to my true self.

To The Sophia Dragon Tribe® for ALWAYS being there to guide and mentor me and in helping me to dig deep and find the strength I needed to bring this book to completion.

To my guides, angels and galactic family, thank you for always being there and for showing me the way.

Thank you Emrys, the more I get to know who I really am the stronger it makes me and the more unconditional love I have for myself and others.

Thank you to Martha and Poppy, my beautiful furry friends who have really taught me what unconditional love is about.

Finally, thank you to all of my friends and family who along the way have been teachers in my journey of self mastery, every moment was a chance to learn.

(Kaia Ra®, The Sophia Code® and The Sophia Dragon Tribe® are registered trademarks of Kaia Ra, LLC. Used with permission).

INTRODUCTION

Global Awakening

What do I mean by awakening? Humankind has lived in a society of inequality, money and material focussed behaviour, wars, being told what to do, how to act, who to love, how to behave and all in a way that kept us from our true selves. The awakening is a realisation that things are not right, that as an individual you have to do something about your life, to make changes that create improvements for yourself but also for others. It is a realisation that what exists in the current reality is not all there is. It is a deep knowing that there is more to life than what can be seen with the human eyes. A coming to know, a remembering that the lack that you have felt in your life is because you are not connected to your true self and no matter how the external circumstances of your life are, only change within is the way to create the life you want. What is happening here is you are raising your consciousness to a higher level.

The slow awakening that has been building over the past 20-30 years got ramped up into high gear in 2012. Since then there have been an increasing number of people starting to realise that change in their life is absolutely necessary, their spirit (or soul) has been calling them into action, for now is the time. The Mayans, amongst others predicted that 2012 was the end of an age and the birth of a new age on earth would begin. There have also been a number of astrological events and planet alignments which have occurred since 2012 to support the raising in the level of consciousness that is occurring on the planet. It is the inner work that all awakened people are doing and will do, making changes for themselves in their mind, body, and spirit balance to bring themselves back to their true self. This will create a shift on planet earth to support the newly dawned Age of Aquarius and bring about the harmony and balance that is so needed.

You may have heard the term lightworker before and this is the name given to a person whose focus is positive, loving, caring and compassionate, who does not give in to fear and works with the light of their spirit (or soul) to bring forth positive outcomes in their lives and in the world around them. When you awaken and begin your journey to self-discovery you too will be working with the light of your spirit (or soul) and will be on your way to becoming a lightworker yourself.

An awakening journey is one of great joy, fun and a discovery of things that have been unseen or hidden previously. It is also a journey of healing and releasing of pain, fear and suffering. It is a journey and not a destination, there are stages, waves, peaks and troughs. It is learning how to handle the different stages and cope with the highs and lows that brings you self-mastery. The ability to be wise enough to know how to deal with the challenges that life on planet earth brings whilst still being able to sit in your true self, being able to manage your thoughts, feelings and emotions and allowing yourself the time to understand them and let them go. It is to actively listen, be self-aware and to positively respond to others rather than reacting. It is a challenging, beautiful, amazing and worthwhile journey!

The Impact of the COVID19 Pandemic

The impact of the COVID19 pandemic on the lives and more importantly the psyche of the population is not to be underestimated. Each of you will have had / be having your own experience whether as a key worker having to change the way in which you work or being told to stay at home and to isolate yourself from everyone but the people you live with. This situation causes most to look at the way that they live, the things that matter to them, to appreciate things that they could no longer do amidst the restrictions being imposed. Some people dipped deeply into fear, fear of getting the virus, fear of dying, fear of other people and so on. Fear is the most destructive of emotions and the impact to those people has been huge, physically, mentally, emotionally and spiritually. If you are reading this book, you probably evaluated your life and began to question things. The value of things in your life probably changed and appreciation came in a much greater way. Having time away from work, away from the treadmill of life will have given you time to take stock and reflect on what you want from your life. The importance of your relationships, whether those relationships are working, if you are happy in your career and so on. You may have faltered or stalled wondering how you are going to make those changes and this is where I can help you with the guidance in this book.

The way in which governments, the media and the public's different reactions to everything that has been unfolding has brought about a view on how our society behaves. The things that are collectively believed, the way in which everyone is expected to act, say, think and do. It has brought about divides in opinion and brought into the light the nature of the pressure on individuals to conform to the collective more than ever before, the restriction of the individual to say and do what they want to, the freedom that was thought to be there and is not, has been seen in its true colours. These revelations have wide reaching ramifications for an awakening person and finding your path to your true self never more important than it is at this moment in time. The more that events in the world shift and change the more that it will challenge belief systems, views of others, the sense of self, one's place in society, and much more. Everything is changing and with change comes uncertainty, uncomfortableness, a sense of feeling adrift, a wanting for things to remain the same or return to how they were before. All of these feelings are natural and it will take a strong heart to walk forth through these changes and keep steadfast on their path whilst having the flexibility to move and change as one's spirit directs. The goal of an awakening person is to find more joy, love and happiness in life and to do this through self love, trust and wisdom. Taking this journey of self-discovery will give you the tools to be able to achieve this even through the chaos of the rebirth of life on earth.

Your Inner Magick

Awakening your inner Magick is a parable. It is awakening the divine, magickal angel that you ARE who is full of unconditional divine love. Following the path of this awakening brings you closer to your true self, helps you to get rid of any false, unworthy ideas about yourself and allows you to walk onto the path of your greatest potential, one that you may not yet be aware of. Your inner Magick is the light of your true being, the source of your own truth, the everything that you could ever hope or dream to be. It is the energy of your divine being that is always there for you every minute of every day of your life, even in the darkest times. This is the journey that you are beginning…………..

Note from the Author

When the idea for this book was forming in my heart and being given to me by my true self, I knew that I wanted to create something that was personal. What you will discover as you read are reflections from my personal journey of discovery. I use my journey because it is authentic. All of the activities, exercises and meditations I have personally used and found deeply helpful in my own awakening journey. You should be able to relate to the situations I describe, you will feel resonance in the core of your being and will recognise that some of these things also true for you. I also provide information and facts from research including from my own doctorate research, observations and learning from myself and others. Religion does not come into anything in this book, it does not matter what faith you have (if any). Most important of all there is a message that comes directly from my heart to yours and each message although perhaps similar in nature will be unique to you. What you will read is my truth, It is not my intention to tell you what to believe, listen to your hearts and fine your own truth within my words.

If you have experienced trauma in your life then I highly recommend that alongside this programme you seek out a professional counsellor who can help you.

How to use this book

With any self-improvement programme, there are two essential components that need to be in place for what my guidance teaches, for it to really work for you. They are:

- A genuine desire or want to change yourself and your life
- A genuine desire to be successful and happy without suffering, without pain and with love.

If like me you have read other books similar to this you may have been left wondering how you are supposed to achieve what was suggested or maybe it was not the right message at the right time for you. If you have tried other self-improvement programmes before and they have not been successful it is likely not to be because of the programme itself but your engagement with it. I have spoken to lots of people who read a book, listen to a podcast, take a class and then expect the information from them to somehow osmotically change them into the fantastic human being that the book, podcast etc sold them. In reality YOU HAVE TO DO THE INNER WORK YOURSELF, IT CAN BE HARD AT TIMES AND CHALLENGING BUT THE REWARDS ARE GREAT. This programme is no different! The other thing I would like to highlight is that there is a right time for you to read and truly hear the words in your heart. You may find you read something and think that it is true for you but you may need to read something many times before your heart hears the truth and you FEEL it within you. Be patient with yourself and keep giving yourself regular reminders until you get that full Ah Ha moment. This may well happen after you have dealt with many layers of pain or wounding that you have healed.

As you read through the section 'Awakening to how your world is' you will find that some or all explanations, scenarios, examples etc will resonate with you. You may find that you have moments of clarity that raise your awareness of your life and develop your awakening further.

In the section "Your Awakening Journey' will take you through the 7 Pillars of Personal Change and how to begin your journey of self-discovery.

In the next section 'Tools to support your Awakening Journey' you will find a wide range of exercises, guided meditations and metaphysical therapies that will support you on your awakening journey. You may be drawn to some rather than others but remember that it is a journey so if some do not seem relevant to you at the beginning that is okay. They may be relevant further into your journey. Do go back and read them again, this section particularly is designed for you to come back to again and again.

As explained you do not necessarily need to do every exercise or meditation, however it is essential to follow the 7 Pillars of Personal Change; doing this will ensure that whichever exercise or meditation you do is the right one for you and will help you to embed the change in your life on a permanent basis. You do not have to be perfect, negative things WILL happen but by using the tools in this book you can choose how you deal with them in a positive way. Personal change does not happen overnight. You can and will have immediate breakthroughs that will leap you forward but there will also be times when you feel that you have stepped backwards. All of this is part of the journey, it is a journey and not a destination. Focus on the journey, on a day by day basis.

In the final section 'Awakening to the magick in your life' you will find guidance on things that will come up for you as you move along your awakening journey including symptoms that may happen for you in your mind, body, and spirit how to use your new found knowing in other areas of your life and how to continue to manage your awakening journey.

My Background

I felt it important to include a little of my background and some key events that led me to really begin my journey of self-discovery. I am not going to make any judgements of myself (or anyone else) as I go along, these are some of the facts about my life as I see them! My childhood was not the easiest for me, from a young age I felt that I was different from everyone else, I have a memory of standing in the playground alone watching the other children play and wondered why I did not seem to fit in. This theme carried on throughout my school life, I was bullied and I am sure that other children felt that I thought I was better than them, this was not the case; I just struggled to relate to them. When school was done I sighed in relief and spent a number of years cocooned within the family unit. There were a number of significant events along the way, doing a fire-walk with Anthony Robbins, travelling and living in Israel and visiting lots of different countries.

Relationships were challenging for me, I now realise that all of the pain of the bullying and feeling so out of place in society had made me close my heart. I actually felt very little, it was like I went about life numb, everything happening around me and me at the centre of the storm. Meeting my wife did change that to an extent, giving me some purpose and helping to think that I was finally living the life that society expected of me.

After a few years settled into married life, working, buying a house etc I started to get restless about the work I was doing, there were parts of the job I loved and others I hated and I soon realised that unless I started to study to qualify in another field I would be stuck in that job for always (not that it was a bad job just not for me). My wife was amazingly supportive if it had not been for her I would never have applied for the first course that I took, my school experience had really left me scared about going back into education. Once I got into the course however I loved the studying and found that I was quite good at it too and so over a period of 8 years I did something in the region of

8 qualifications including my MBA. I also changed jobs and started teaching at the college I studied at.

There were concurrent themes in my life. At work I was complimented on my ability to understand people, I knew what to say at the right time, was empathetic and had a good understanding of human behaviour and these are the foundations that this book is built upon. The other theme was a personal one; throughout my life I had battled with self-esteem, why did the other kids not like me at school? Why did I not think I was good enough to get a girlfriend? Why was I not good enough for that promotion? Why did I think I could not study and achieve? Why, why, why? You get the picture I am sure!

By 2013 I was teaching, had all these qualifications, had hit 40 and survived (Lol!) and my life seemed to be okay. My wife and I travelled a lot to the USA and things ticked along, however underneath all of this there was an underlying unhappiness, I felt I was going through the motions. Work consumed a lot of my time and I felt tired a lot, I was in a rut, on the treadmill of life, I started to really question, is this it? I would often spend time daydreaming about what life might be like if some things were different, I thought that moving abroad would make things better for example.

My wife had suffered some ill health for a while but in 2013 life events took over and she suffered a number of strokes and then was diagnosed with breast cancer. Talk about rocket me into some life-changing situations, I wanted change and I got change and I was not happy with it at all. However these changes were the catalyst for the journey of self-discovery I then started to take. The ride, roller-coaster does not begin to describe it!

The strokes totally changed my wife's behaviour and I began to see 3 different personalities, I had to start to cope with the different ones and this was a huge learning curve. The strokes happened within months of each other and just as she was recovering from one she'd have another, then the breast cancer diagnosis happened and the treatment for that began. During this time I also discovered that some of the strokes and delayed cancer diagnosis were as a result of medical negligence and I began litigation. In 2015 I gave up my job as a lecturer to care full-time. This was all totally life-changing as you can imagine and to me I had two clear paths I could take, the route of depression and mental health issues or to use the experiences to grow and develop myself and start moving into some of my potential as a human being; I did the latter. My awakening journey has changed and developed me in many ways including, a calmness within, a very positive view on life, an open and much wider perspective on reality. I have considerably increased self-love, have a clearer focus on my life purpose, a contentedness and peace within. I have also increased my psychic abilities and developed my abilities in clairaudience, clairvoyance, claircognizance, clairsentience, mediumship and empathic abilities.

Support for your Awakening Journey

Going through an awakening journey alone can be done but it is a lot easier if you have someone who you can speak to about it and share your experiences. If you have a friend who is going through a similar journey or someone who has awakened before you then speak to them about being able to regularly share what you are going through. I found having mentors a vital part of my personal journey.

Journalling

In Pillar 3 of the change process, making sense, (see your awakening journey section) I recommend writing down what you have learned from a part of that step. Keeping a regular journal is a great way of working out your feelings, identifying issues and bringing things forth from your subconscious mind. I resisted a lot at first at the idea of journalling but when I started to do it on a regular basis I found it immensely helpful.

You can write a journal by hand, there are lots of lovely journal books available to buy or you can create a document on your computer if you find typing easier than writing by hand.

Before you start to journal take a few minutes to do the breathing exercises on page 97 and then either focus on a particular issue that you are dealing with or wanting to bring forward OR Just allow yourself to start typing / writing and see what comes forth. You may be amazed at what you write if you simply allow it to flow. The insights from the journal can be very powerful and will help you to create the changes you want in your life. The journal can also be a good record for you to come back to in order to remind yourself of what came through if you get stuck or fall off the 'wagon' or to show you how well you are doing and as a record of your journey.

Core Skills for Awakening

Self-Reflection

The ability to look within is a core skill for this process, it is a journey and the more you reflect the better you get at it. If self-reflection is not something that you are used to doing then setting aside time on a daily basis to reflect on the day, before bed may be a good idea. One way of helping to reflect is by journalling. Writing down your reflections can be a powerful way of raising your self-awareness and helping you to identify what you need to work on.

Self-Honesty

Being super honest with yourself is vital to any self-improvement process, this is not always easy. It is important not to go into self-judgement when this occurs; and you may find that you have "Ah ha" moments when you realise patterns of behaviour. The following step is to then take responsibility for yourself and not place the blame on others. This is often harder than it sounds particularly if shifting the responsibility of events and actions in your life is a pattern of behaviour for you.

Visualisation Techniques

- Close your eyes and take a few moments to relax where you are sitting or laying and let your breathing settle into a comfortable rhythm.
- Try to be inside the experience rather than looking from the outside in.
- Create a mental picture of the environment you are in, where are you? Indoors or outdoors? What is the floor like and the walls if inside. If you're outside what is the ground like and the surroundings, what sounds do you hear? Is it hot or cold? Is it windy, noisy or quiet?
- What do you see? Build the picture of what you see, the colours, shapes etc
- Can you smell anything? Can you taste anything?
- Touch – what does the seat or bed feel like, your clothes, the texture of the material

- Create the emotions related to the visualisation – what do you feel? Allow yourself to feel and recognise the emotions.
- Do not JUDGE the situation as you are simply experiencing it.
- To end the visualisation think about something you like, such as a favourite food, and return to the present moment.

Communication

Communication is an interesting thing to talk about. A lot of people think of the words we say but communication goes a whole lot further than just words. There have been many different theories of communication, the following is mine which is based on personal experience working with many people over the years and channelled information.

Words:

The actual words that are said form only 7 % of the total communication and when communicating with two people who do not share the same first language or Mother tongue this percentage is reduced. This is also why the written word in non business communications can also be easily misconstrued.

Tonality:

The way that words are said form 13% of the communication that is happening, the exact same words can have completely different connotations and meaning when said in a different way.

Body Language:

Often people think that body language is shown through the folding of arms and the touching of the face, as common examples, but body language is much more complex. Body language is how people express how they are feeling without verbalising their emotions. It is automatic responses to the other person's words, tone, and body language, and psychic information. Being more aware and present will help to not only notice your own body language but also the body language of others. This can be vitally important in being successful in relationships both personal and professional.

Psychic information:

This is where my model differs from others, we all transmit and receive psychic information from other people. We connect with one another's energy fields and as thoughts and emotions are thought and felt they are then transmitted to another person psychically. We can ALL read energy. Think of a time when you have walked into a room and "felt or sensed" the atmosphere in the room, this is you reading the psychic energy of the room. We all pick up on this information and act and react to it accordingly, often without realising how or why we know the information. The transmission of psychic information relates directly to the creation of your own personal reality, if you think negative thoughts, feel negative emotions then you project them outwards through your own psychic transmission. This transmission is received by others and the universe (which is responsible for things outside your control, so-called coincidences, synchronicities etc). This psychic information that you transmit is then used in conjunction with the universe to create the life you are living. This is why the management of thoughts and emotions through the practices that I am teaching in this book are vital to the creation of a happier life. Key messages here is that YOU are in control and can change the life you have now and that energy follows thoughts and emotions, your life is what you think and feel!

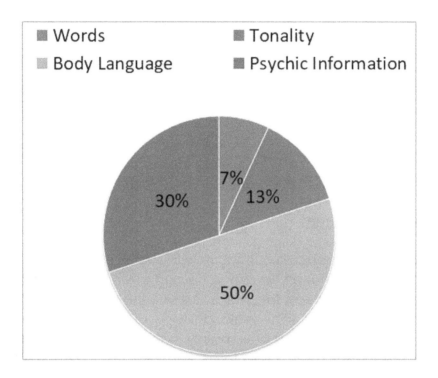

Circles of Discovery

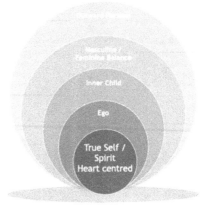

Circles of Discovery

This is the face that is put on for society, the conforming to the 'norm' the fitting in with what is expected, it is also the false self, the fearful self, the seeker of answers outside of oneself, this persona lives mainly in the mind

Inner child is the part of our consciousness that contains our wounding from childhood and the holder of our innocence and creative genius

Masculine / Feminine Balance

Inner Child

Ego

True Self / Spirit Heart centred

The masculine and feminine balance what is needed to bring forth all parts of our nature, the feminine creative power and the masculine that manifests

The ego is the protector of the physical self, based in the mind, includes the internal critic

Outward Persona

The outward persona is fitting in with societal norm, it's the face that you put on for everyone and often even yourself. This is the fearful self, the wounded self, the self in pain, the false self, the self that seeks answers outside of oneself. The outward persona lives mainly in the mind, often lacks critical thinking, is happier to be told what to do and think by authority, often believes what they read in newspapers or what the mainstream media says, doesn't question or challenge what scientists say, when critical thinking does occur it is limited to anything that can only be "proven". This is also where a false sense of spirituality exists, people who think they are spiritual and say all the right things but do not do the inner work, they may be kind to others but NOT to themselves and often harbour deep self-loathing and have extreme self-esteem issues.

Masculine & Feminine Balance

I explain in detail about masculine and feminine balance later in the book. In short, this is the balance needed in everyone, no matter their gender. Masculine and feminine balance is required to be fully whole. If you want to reach your potential as human being or as a spiritual being living a physical life, this balance will help you achieve it. It will also enable you to get the best out of relationships with others. This balance prevents the need to seek something that is lacking within from another person and this enables healthy relationships and the ability to be fully creative and turn ideas into reality.

Inner Child

Again I go into detail about inner child later in the book. In short, inner child is the part of our consciousness that contains wounding from our childhood, this is when our innocence did not realise the way that the world worked or how humans behave and was wounded as a result. It also holds the consciousness and memories of any abuse that we may have suffered. Inner child is also where our absolute innocence is and our creative genius.

Ego

The ego is the protector of the physical self, it is based in the mind and is also the internal critic. The ego seeks to protect us at all costs which can often be to our detriment particularly if there is a lack of balance with the heart and the true self.

True Self

The true self is where the spirit or soul lives, it is who we really are. It provides the conscious mind (if listened to) with accurate information and guidance about how to live. It guides us on our life path and is the short cut to learning life lessons and fulfilling karma. This is the heart space, the heart energy, the heart mind. Too much have we been told that we should not lead from our hearts but use our minds and that is not true. The heart is not over emotional. It is the place where divine knowledge pours through and brings about wisdom on how to be who you really are. If you live from this space you will tap into the law of attraction, you will create the life that you deserve and desire. We do experience times when we are our true selves but these moments are often short and when we are dealing with life issues we go back to the outward persona, the ultimate goal is to be the true self all the time. This does not mean that we won't experience negativity or challenges but it does mean that how we handle them will be much better. The circles of discovery are there to teach that to get from the outward persona to the true self one has to work to create a masculine and feminine balance, needs to recognise and heal the inner child and needs to create a balance between the ego and the heart. All of the activities, exercises and meditations in this book are there to help you go through the circles, as you discover yourself in each one you will get closer to being in your true self all of the time.

AWAKENING TO HOW YOUR WORLD IS

How is your Life Anyway?

How do you identify with yourself? When people ask you about yourself you probably answer with where you were born, what your job or career is, whether you are married or not, whether you have any children or not etc The majority of people are living their lives according to what other people think their lives should be. Most people are living lives that are a lie and are not being their true selves.

You are a consciousness experiencing your life through a physical body! Finding your way back to your true self will enable you to live the life that your heart desires.

Our whole lives are a lists of continual conditioning and brainwashing. From the moment we are born we are given the conditions and norms that our parents or caregivers have. We are then given the same at school, told what is normal and not normal, what is right and wrong, what we should or should not do. Some of these lessons we need, like not stealing or killing someone else for example but much of what we are taught limits our thinking and limits what is possible for us to achieve in our lives. Many of the metaphysical teachings in

1

this book are criticised, ridiculed and dismissed as nonsense because the ideas do not fit into the norm that we are taught. None of this conditioning allows us to become our true selves, indeed it pushes us to create the outward personas that are our false selves and encourage us to live lives according to what everyone else thinks, according to the norm. You see, anyone that is deemed in anyway different, for example someone who has a different sexual expression is often ridiculed or bullied. In some areas of the population tolerance is better but often there is still the check against the norm.

I am a big observer of people, and there are some very common themes to many people's lives, consider the life of an average working, married mother:

The alarm goes off, Mum gets up, makes sure the children are up, goes downstairs, makes breakfast and packed lunches, sees her partner off to work, takes the kids to school, and goes to her own place of work. She does her job, leaves work, picks up the kids, does some shopping, goes home, cooks dinner with her partner, supports the children with their homework, eats, watches TV, and puts the children to bed, and it's wine o'clock. More TV, showers and goes to bed. She gets into bed and can't get to sleep because her mind won't switch off. Her mind is saying to her "Finally I have your attention!"

We are also operating according to conditioning and norms when we drive to or from work and don't remember the journey, when we misinterpret information or communication from others leading to mistakes or arguments, when we become distracted and miss out and when we don't remember things that happened, or tasks to be done.

These are just a couple of examples, but many people experience similar scenarios in their lives and feel like they are on treadmills or hamster wheels going through the motions rather than living real lives. Most of the time they are working to pay the bills and there seems to be very little time left to actually enjoy being a human being. Moments of joy or happiness are often fleeting and quite often induced using some sort of stimulant such as alcohol, cigarettes, medication, drugs and food to name a few. There are other times that joy occurs but it is usually when love is involved, falling in love with a partner, loving one's family or children and so on. Sadly, unconditional love is sorely lacking in most people's lives.

This treadmill or hamster wheel is known in mindfulness as being on autopilot, where the focus is doing, it is task-based and future-focused, If you are on autopilot you are not present in the moment. The impact of this? High levels of stress that lead to physical illness, missing out on beautiful moments in life such as, precious time with your children, your partner or other loved ones, and a tendency to use external stimuli to make you feel better. External stimuli include:

- Smoking
- Excessive alcohol
- Painkillers
- Extreme exercise
- High adrenaline activities
- Shopping and the attainment of material items
- Becoming involved emotionally with soap operas or reality TV shows
- Chocolate or other processed sugar items
- Being excessively busy, a lot of people feel guilty stopping and doing nothing

What is the cause of our unhappiness in life? Our constant attempts to achieve the next thing that will make us feel good? The search outside of ourselves instead of searching and healing within? There is one simple answer, fear. Fear is more often than not an illusion created by our ego, Fear is false evidence appearing real.

We live in a harsh world where hurt, wounding and pain are common place and emotions are suppressed. We spend so much time being busy and fearful of feeling the pain of our wounding that all the trauma gets suppressed.

A lot of people know that their lives are not right and that they are not happy but are at a loss as to what they can do about it. Indeed many people believe they have no or little control over their lives.

If you stop and listen to what your heart is saying you may find that the message is that you are dissatisfied with your life and you may recognise some of the external stimuli that you are using discussed above. You may also find that you are bored with your life. Boredom can lead to escapism and number of behaviours Including:

- Overeating or snacking / picking food
- Excessive use of TV, internet, social media
- Excessive use of computer games
- Watching pornography
- Excessive exercising
- Excessive daydreaming

Boredom in relationships can often lead to extra-relationship affairs, use of prostitutes, and excessive working to name a few.

Can you see the cycle? Fear and societal circumstances lead to abuse of the mind, body, and spirit and a disconnection from the true self. Suppressed emotions and pain lead to physical symptoms and manifest as illness in the body including anything from physical pain to mild symptoms like headaches and stomach upsets to more serious autoimmune diseases, and cancer. The mind, body, and spirit balance is further damaged by chemical medications given to "treat" the problem. These medications are sticky plasters that often causes side effects and addiction. The root cause of the problem is not dealt with by medical professionals. The health systems do not look at the emotional, mental, and spiritual reasons why someone is ill. Breaking this cycle is a big part of the awakening journey to heal past pain and wounding and to journey to the true self.

Mind, Body, and Spirit

As human beings we are mind, body, and spirit. To be our true selves, to obtain the love, joy and happiness we so desire, we need a balance between our minds, bodies, and spirits.

The human mind processes all of the information sent to it by all the senses. It manages the body, it is a storehouse for memories. The mind is the home of the ego which is the body's protector and where our intellectual intelligence is. When the mind, body, and spirit is balanced there is a superhighway between the intellectual mind and the heart mind. On this road there is a beautiful exchange of information that allows for rounded, complete information and allows you to make good decisions to live your life.

We often neglect and abuse he physical vessel that carries us through our lives. Its perfect design is there to enable us to live our lives in the way that we are meant to. However we frequently abuse the body, feeding it poor food, not moving it to ensure all working parts stay working, putting chemicals in it and damaging it with harmful thought processes. In their book The Healing Self Deepak Chopra and Rudolph Tanzi argue that the mind and the body are intrinsically connected. They write that,"the 'mind' is spread throughout the body and indeed each cell communicates with others in ensuring the health of the whole physical body." They go on to explain that "it doesn't matter that the mind-body is invisible because at the molecular level it isn't. There are enough chemical clues to convince anyone that mood, beliefs, expectations, fears, memories, pre*dispositions, habits and old conditioning, all at the centre of the mind and are critical to a person's health*." (14-15)

Chopra and Tanzi's research is important in understanding how your own mind and body work and the impact that the way you think and live has on your quality of life.

A simple exercise here can easily prove this point. If you sit quietly and then think about something really bad that has happened to you, almost immediately you can feel a physiological response in your body, some form of discomfort or pain. Equally if you think about something that makes you very happy you can get a feeling in your body that is usually a good sensation. Anyone who has had a job interview can relate to this, the thoughts about being judged, being good enough, and getting the job can cause a lot of physical symptoms such as stomach ache, frequent need to use the toilet, headache, and dry mouth.

Now when we talk about spirit what does that conjure in your mind, in your heart? Spirit is that sometimes unknown part of you, that intangible essence of who you are, the thing that is just out of reach or gets buried beneath a mountain of life. Spirit is the essence of who you really are, that unknown you, that known you, that person who longs to come out more often, that core that you want to be all the time. In metaphysics it is described as the part of the source of all life within you, the part that is connected to everything and everyone in the universe. Much of our suffering is caused by not believing in or being disconnected from that source and the universe and each other.

The need for Balance

Mind, body, and spirit balance:

In order to be in balance there needs to be a synergistic flow of energy between the mind, body, and spirit. That flow is continuous and moves freely; no element (mind, body or spirit) takes priority. Each is equally important and each needs to be nurtured and nourished to maintain that balance.

To create balance, the most important place to start with is the mind. Most of us are addicted to overthinking and the balance between our thoughts and intuition is weighted heavily in favour of our minds. Most of us are taught to use our minds, to logically think things through, to use our intellect to solve problems, to only trust in what we can tangibly reconcile and understand with our minds. Much of today's education revolves around the need for proof that something is real or exists and the concept of critical thinking does not extend to intuition as this is not seen as tangible. The body needs to be nourished and moved and treated with respect and the spirit needs to be listened to and honoured.

When do you feel most alive?

Most of us have snatches of times when we feel most alive, most connected to our lives, the earth, each other and between our mind, body, and spirit. But sadly for a lot of people these moments are rare or do not last. What and

7

when are your moments? Think carefully about them, who are you with? Are you alone? Where are you? How do you feel? What are you thinking? What else is happening within and around you?

For me it is when I am with nature, with people I love, with animals, when I am watching a great movie, when exercising. It is also when I learn something new, but now I have learned to expand that, to change that and now it is quite different. I get to feel more alive when dealing with even small often mundane things, I appreciate all of the facets of living a human life.

How do you see the world?

For eons people have asked the question what is the meaning of life? What do you think? I have always had a simple answer, to love and to learn. But how do we know what we know? Where does that knowledge come from? We learn from being a baby but how much of your life has been or is influenced and conditioned by society and the opinions and attitudes of your caregivers as a child?

I started to realise that for most of my life I was being told what to think and feel and there seemed to be no space for what **I think and feel!** I realised that many people, myself included are or were living a life based on what other people expect or expected. That there were limitations put on what to do, where to go, who to see, how to behave based on things external too oneself. With this knowledge it is no wonder that as individuals we fight for and want to control everything; that we never seem to be happy and always look for something wrong. That we often have a negative view of the world as we see it. We are not being our true selves and the reality is that many of us are lost and do not know who our true selves are.

8

We all see the world differently, we all live in our own version of the world and often this is why people struggle to see eye to eye, why other people's viewpoints can seem alien to us. There is one common thread that tie us all together in our worlds and that is unconditional love. Unconditional love breaks though everything. Most of us are very good at giving love to others, at being compassionate and caring towards others however most of us are NOT good at loving ourselves, at being compassionate and caring towards ourselves. Understanding that other people do not see the world in quite the same way that we do can help us considerably in our relationships with others. Taking a moment to zoom out and see the other person's perspective and then zooming back in to the detail of the moment can really help to bring greater understanding and compassion for others and bring wiser and wider knowledge about yourself in the process. How else do we view our world? Most of us believe in what we SEE with our eyes, what we can touch, hear, taste, and smell. We base our thoughts and opinions mainly on the 5 senses. Science tells us if something does not follow a certain rule then it cannot be, our logical human mind has to make sense of something, pigeon hole it, compartmentalise it for it to FEEL comfortable, this is the ego mind making things feel safe for you. Yet millions of people believe in various religions and in a common concept of existence of and survival after death of the spirit, yet we cannot see it and science cannot prove it (yet). How many of you use sayings such as " what goes around comes around" and believe it to be true? What does that say about your belief system and how you view the world? Karma as the saying is referring to, who is it that ensures that it happens? There are many examples of how we believe something that cannot be proven by science. The point here is for you to go beyond what you believe with your five senses and start thinking and feeling what you get with your 6th sense. Commonly reference to the 6th sense relates to psychic ability however I am referring to your intuition, your gut instinct, that sense of knowing something that you cannot quite explain (which is a type of psychic ability).

Taking Responsibility for your Own Life

This is a VERY IMPORTANT element, taking responsibility for you life including all of the things you feel you have done wrong, the current state of your relationships, finances, and health is vital in the process of self-improvement. However this is not a blame yourself and feel sorry for yourself exercise either. It is about being honest about how things are and not blaming other people for it. We always have free will choices including choosing our reactions to situations and people. This does not mean that being abused by someone is right for example. However there are some situations where someone who is being abused enables their abuser or allows the abuse to continue. I know this from personal experience and I told myself, first time it happened was the other person's responsibility, the second time it happened it was my responsibility. I know I allowed abuse to happen for many years, it did not make it right and of course the perpetrator should not have done it to me however I take responsibility for allowing it to continue, I do not beat myself up about it, I am just accepting it and I am taking back control.

Taking responsibility also means that you do not engage in manipulative behaviour that is wrapped up as trying to be nice or helping people and example of this is below:

Many of us make sacrifices for other people, friends and loved ones, we give up something we want to do or somewhere we want to go but do we do it with an open heart? With love for the person or people we are sacrificing for? Are we sacrificing for the right reasons? Or are we allowing others to control and manipulate us? If you do sacrifice for someone else just remember it is YOUR decision, YOUR choice, so do it with the full knowledge and understanding that either you are giving in to control and manipulation and allowing it to happen OR you are sacrificing with a full loving heart for the other person. Many of us sacrifice for others and then blame them or regret that we did it, secretly wishing that we had not, that we had done what we desired to do and when this happens something else occurs. We then create a situation where we "get our own back" on the other person, "make them pay" for stopping us doing what we wanted. This is often achieved subconsciously and in subtle ways, we go into a bad mood and don't speak, we sulk, we withdraw kindness or loving gestures, go off sex for the night(or a week). The list is endless and only limited by our imagination but you get the idea. This is another example of taking responsibility for your actions; DO NOT make a sacrifice and then "make the other person pay" you may as well not have bothered. Either do it with love in your heart or DON'T DO IT AT ALL.

I have seen lots of people I know engage in such behaviour without even realising what they are doing, it is subtle and underhanded controlling behaviour and is definitely not taking responsibility! Much of this type of behaviour can be caused by a lack of balance of mind, body, and spirit and a lack of balance in ones masculine and feminine energies.

Addiction

It's funny when you talk about addiction most people do not think about themselves, they think about others, hard drug addicts or alcoholics and think that it is someone else's problem but almost everyone is addicted to something. In the world as it is today there are so many things that people can become addicted to, we all know about nicotine in cigarettes and caffeine in coffee, tea and soft drinks and maybe chocolate! The reality though is that most people are addicted to processed sugars, they mess around with the human body's processes so much that we 'need' them all the time. We end up in sugar yoyo where we get highs and lows that physically affect how we feel giving us a sugar rush (high) and then a tired, lethargic shaky feeling (low). The brain also sees sugar as a reward and if that is reinforced by emotional eating for reward (I worked hard so I deserve a bar of chocolate or a bag of chips) this can be a hard habit to break. Sugar is practically in every processed food and of course fruit and some vegetables too. The difference with the sugar in fruits is it reacts differently in the body. White bread, pasta and the like are also broken down into glucose in the body quickly and contribute to the sugar fix. Making dietary changes and being mindful in your eating (discussed later) will help you to break a cycle of sugar addiction.

What about prescription drugs? How many of you have been on the same medication for years? Does your GP review whether you still need it? Is it that your body is so used to getting the medication that you can't do without it even though it is no longer helping? How many of you take pain killers regularly? Ones' with codeine in are particularly addictive, do you find yourself needing a painkiller, particularly at certain times? Painkillers if used on a regular basis can actually cause you to feel pain it is how the addiction works. Do not try to come off any prescribed medication without the guidance of your healthcare practitioner however it is well worth a medication review with them to see if the drug is still needed and if there are any alternatives including homeopathic remedies.

If you 'need' your morning cup of coffee or tea to get you going you are probably addicted to the caffeine in them. Certain painkillers contain high amounts of caffeine that can also give highs and lows if taken regularly. High amounts of caffeine can cause symptoms such as fast heart rate, insomnia, nausea and upset stomach, feelings of anxiousness, and headache to name a few. The FDA (USA) and the NHS (UK) say that up to 4 cups of coffee a day is okay for you. Don't be fooled by decaffeinated drinks either they have less caffeine but still contain it and of course cola and energy drinks also contain caffeine. Withdrawal from personal experience can be terrible and should be done gradually. You may suffer extreme tiredness, headaches, night tremors, restless legs, anxiety and nervousness.

What about alcohol? It's funny that reading Facebook posts of friends, mainly women that post regularly about their need for a glass of wine to unwind and I see many jokes about needing Prosecco on tap. I wonder how many of you "need" wine or other forms of alcohol to unwind and relax, how many glasses are needed and how often? Is it once a week or every night and how many at a time? When does this turn from "I like a glass of wine" to "I need a glass of wine"? When does it become an addiction? I am not judging anyone but you ask yourself, is that you?

Let us talk about the most addictive thing of all that I would guess 98% of people are addicted to today, over thinking. How many of you just cannot switch off your brain to unwind and relax and to go to sleep well? Overthinking can come in many guises, worry is the most common and I will address this later on in more detail. Thinking of too many different things and not focusing on what is going on in the current moment. Going from one task to another without completing any fully; I call this the butterfly effect.

In today's world we do many things to stop the overthinking process, watching TV, exercise or team sports, reading, crafts, anything we enjoy that focuses our minds on something other than what is going on in our heads! What do you do?

Whatever your addiction, evaluate how much it is impacting your mind, body, and spirit balance. Be honest with yourself and if you are addicted to a number of things then try giving up one thing at a time and always ask your healthcare practitioner for advice.

Judgement of Self and Others

We live in a judgemental society and people make judgements about themselves and others almost all the time. Where do these judgements come from?

Some societal judgements include:

- Religious
- Work or career
- How people look and dress
- What people eat
- Where people live
- People's partner's (or not having a partner) & sexual orientation
- Educational background
- Social background (or so-called class)
- Disability including mental health
- Cultural and ethnicity

As I discussed before we all have our own individual view of the things and often people are stuck in their own 'world' and struggle to see things from others perspectives. Using some of the activities in this book can help with this. Judging others shows a lack in yourself, most often this is to make yourself feel better than other people because of a lack of self-esteem. Having a rigid view of societal conditioning makes people feel that everyone has to be the same as them or similar to them otherwise they are not acceptable. We see this in cultural differences, ethnocentrism is widespread in many nations and this leads to further judgement of others who are not of the same cultural background or nationality. This lack of tolerance in the differences we have between each other causes a lot of the issues we see in the world. Being able to recognise that we are all different, respecting those differences and celebrating the things that we share in common are great ways to stop yourself from judging others. Also acceptance that other people will judge you no matter what you say or do and being okay with that will also help you to become happier. The acknowledgement that others judge also allows you to make allowances for this in certain situations such as dressing for a job interview for example. Judgement of others is ultimately a judgement of yourself and is usually linked to some form of insecurity, hurt or wounding that you have endured.

Self-judgement is linked to a lack of self-esteem and a lack of self-love, negative self-talk as a result of trauma, inner child wounding and societal judgements.

Present, Past, and Future

The core of mindfulness which I refer to frequently talks about being present and so it is pertinent to talk about the past and the future.

Past - We often feel defined by the experiences of our past, and believe that those experiences have made us the people we are in the present. To an extent this is true, the lessons of our lives, if we have learned them can make us stronger, more resilient and better people, however bad things that have happened to us tend to linger and cause us pain, this can also manifest in physical illness. Being on autopilot for the majority of the time means that there is no time to be present with the feelings and emotions that you experienced in the past and so they are bottled up and not released. In the longterm this can lead to many of the autoimmune dis-eases that are present today and others such as cancer.

We also have an 'emotional storehouse', this is a memory bank of emotions that are connected to particular experiences from our past. When we are on autopilot and not fully present it is our default to go into this 'emotional storehouse' and match a current experience with a past one. The problem with this response is that we are assuming and or jumping to conclusions about the present experience and can fail to understand and know what is actually happening. This can lead to a distortion of the facts and the truth of what is happening and at worst can cause breakdowns in communication, anxiety, stress, and unhappiness.

Future - In reality the future never actually exists and the past did not happen in the past it happened in the present moment (past present moments), so the only thing that exists is this present moment.

Eckhart Tolle in his groundbreaking book The Power of Now explains this concept well, 'Nothing ever happened in the past; it happened in the now. Nothing will ever happen in the future; it will happen in the now.'

If you are experiencing anxiety or worrying; this is about a future that will in sense never come. Many people create an array of different scenarios about the future, one more terrible than the other and get themselves into such a deep state of fear that they make themselves physically ill.

This does not mean that you cannot make plans and set intentions for the future. The actions that you take in this present moment will help you to create each present moment as we go through linear time. I will discuss how we create our lives later, however it is important to note here that whatever we do in this present moment is setting the energy and intention for each consecutive present moment. If you create negativity (through thoughts and emotions) in the present moment, you will attract negativity back to you in consecutive present moment.

In addition to being on autopilot what else is the cause of this behaviour?

Our minds have been in control for far too long, we have been taught not to trust gut instinct or heart-based decisions because they are 'emotional' and not likely to bring us good decisions. Not everyone believes that or purely uses the mind but when we go into fear it is the mind that takes control and when overthinking really goes into light speed. The majority of people are addicted to overthinking.

Ego :

I have explained that the ego is the protector of the physical body but if you ask the average person what ego is, they will probably say that 'Ego is when someone is arrogant and too full of themselves'. In reality the ego is there to protect you from harm, and It is also how you interact with the world around you as an individual unique person. The challenge with the protection part of the ego is that when you are on autopilot, using your emotional storehouse and focusing on an array of possible futures the ego believes that you are in more danger than you actually are. This puts your body into fight or flight mode and triggers a number of mental and physiological responses, some common ones include :

- Gastrointestinal issues including acid reflux
- Headaches
- Backache
- Chest tightness
- Feeling sick
- Blurry vision
- Very shallow breathing
- Pins and needles in hands and toes
- Bad thoughts about yourself or others

People commonly take over the counter medication for these symptoms and if they get worse then consult a doctor who may prescribe prescription drugs to help. The problem with this is that they only mask the root cause of the issue and put chemicals into the body that it does not know how to deal with. Prescribed drugs also commonly cause other side effects that require further medication and this can spiral out of control. To help the ego to feel that you are safe it requires you to be present, in the present moment for the majority of the time. To make decisions whilst being present that are based on what is actually happening at the time. For there to be dialogue between your heart and your mind that you act upon to keep you safe and happy. Achieving this however is not always easy but some of the activities shown later on in the book will help you to do this.

Energy

What is energy? You may initially think of it as what runs your smart phone or computer but it is much more than that. Everything is energy; all that we see and don't see, all that we touch, all that we 'sense' is energy. Why is this important? We create energy with everything that we do, what we think, and what we feel. Cause and effect....

The same happens with your actions, your emotions and your thoughts, what you think and feel (cause) has an effect in your life. So what does this mean for you? It means if you regularly think bad, negative thoughts and emotions that is what you will get in your life. There are different frequencies of energy; hate, fear, jealousy, and judging (whether towards yourself or others) for example have a low vibrational frequency that brings forth negative energy. We are human and such emotions are part of our journey, however staying in such emotions on a regular basis means that you will stay in a low vibrational energy frequency. The impact of this is that you will be dealing with other low vibration energies that brings experiences like arguments, resentments, misunderstandings, obstacles in your path of life, unhelpful situations, and so on. The more that you move forward into love, compassion, and humility etc, the more it will bring forth higher vibrational frequency energy that will bring you all of the things that you desire for you life. Everything has a vibrational frequency. Animals for example have a very high vibrational frequency and this is why we feel so good around them. It is important that you understand this as I will refer to this in different sections throughout the book.

The Human Energy Field

Once you understand that everything is energy, it makes sense to realise that the human body has an energy field, in fact it has a number of energy fields. Barbara Ann Brennan discusses that there are 7 levels of the human energy field and they can be further expanded to higher levels with spiritual development. Brennan describes the human energy field as 'fields or emanations from the human body.' She goes on to say that the layers of the aura connect to various energy centres throughout the human body, in eastern teachings these are called chakras. There are seven major chakras through the human body, the crown at the top of the head, the third eye centred in the middle forehead, the throat, the heart, the solar plexus which is positioned just above the belly button, the sacral chakra positioned below the belly button and the root chakra positioned at the base of the spine. These major and other minor chakras across the body are the opening points for energy to flow in and out of the body, the flow of this energy is vitally important for the health of a person and the contribution to mind, body, and spirit balance. If some or all of the chakras are blocked it can cause severe disruption to the well being of a person. Think about what happens to water, it has to go somewhere, if water gets blocked then it finds somewhere to go. It floods or overflows; also if water does not flow, does not move then it becomes stagnant and this is what happens with energy in the body. If your chakras are blocked the energy backs up, it becomes stagnant and comes out in physical and mental health problems. Blocking is caused by negativity, poor thought patterns, suppressed emotions, receiving negativity from others, to name a few. The flow of energy through the chakras helps us to express ourselves through our thoughts, emotions and feelings and helps to maintain good physical and mental health. If they are blocked then the opposite occurs and this can lead to serious problems if they continue to be blocked for a long time. This is also what causes a disconnection between body, mind, and spirit, and a disconnection from the wider universe, the earth, animals and our true self. We become dislodged and it makes us feel very alone and this brings deep unhappiness and can lead to depression and other serious mental health problems.

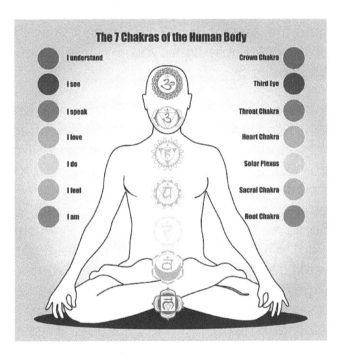

The Assemblage Point

The Assemblage Point is the very centre of the human electromagnetic field. Here, a vortex emerges and life force energy is able to enter the electromagnetic body. This point is normally located on the breast bone. The exact location and angle of entry depend on the physical and mental health of the person. These have a direct effect on a person's energy and are linked to activity in the body's organs, glands, and the brain. This means that behaviour, feelings, and health of every human being directly affects the location and angle

21

of entry of the Assemblage Point and the other way around. The Assemblage Point is a part of the energy body, or aura, around the physical body. It travels from a point normally around the chest through to the back. It may be felt or seen by some people as energy lines concentrating into one point of the body. It may look like a bright area of energy and usually has a diameter of 1 cm where it meets the body. Some people may experience tenderness on the skin at the point where the Assemblage Point enters the body, and if you touch this point quite firmly, you may feel it through to its continuation point on your back.

Native tribes and ancient cultures across the world are aware of the knowledge and importance of the assemblage point in diagnosing illnesses however it is not until recently that wider acknowledgement of the Assemblage Point has happened. In 1996, four detailed articles about the Assemblage Point were published in Positive Health magazine. In August 2000 Dr Angela Blaen was the very first person to have the existence of her Assemblage Point scientifically verified and measured. Practitioners of Assemblage Point alignment consider the Assemblage Point as the missing link to resolving emotional, physical, spiritual, and mental health problems and consider the Assemblage Point an important reason why so many people continue to suffer without a solution for their painful, recurring or continuous symptoms and their negative influence on peoples' Quality of Life.

There are many reasons why a person's Assemblage Point may be out of position. Shock and trauma, divorce and bereavement, drugs or alcohol addiction, infection, surgical operations, childbirth, accidents, illness, violence and intimidation, rape, hunger and thirst can all cause it to either drop or lift out of its normal position. Some people may have an idea that they experienced some kind of change inside following one of these events, but are unable to bring about a return to their former selves via self-reasoning, medication, or therapy. Many people in today's society have an Assemblage Point that is slightly to the right. The left brain processes logical thought, as opposed to creative processes in the right brain. People with busy lifestyles, using a lot of physical and mental energy, would have an active left brain, and this would move their Assemblage Point to the right.

Key message here is your assemblage point needs to be in the right place for optimum health!

The recognition of the need to treat the energetic body as well as the physical body has not been made by most mainstream medical professionals in the West and so is often the reason why the root cause of illnesses are not identified by such practitioners.

Reincarnation - why its true!

Research by the International Metaphysical Ministry (IMM) indicates that over two thirds of the world population believe in reincarnation. I have a very practical view on this and why this is true.

If we were here to only live the life we have and when we died that was it, we would learn very little and there would be good cause to feel 'what is the point.' There would be little room for making mistakes, little scope for experiencing a range of places, people, professions, hobbies etc and most of this would be based on your socio-economic situation usually the one you are born into. The family you have (or don't), the partner (or not), children (or not), you get the picture, it is all very limiting. Living just one life does not explain how some people are good at some things and not others, does not explain the plethora of examples of children who remember and can describe a past (or parallel) life or life on the other side or heaven or other dimension. Reincarnation helps to explain and come to terms with the death of a child or young person instead of the futility of it. If you are in any doubt as to whether or not you believe in reincarnation then analyse your own life, the people you know, go deep into your intuition and let it guide you to the answer.

Life Plans and Lessons and Repeating Patterns

Earth is a university, it has been the Oxford or Harvard of the universe for thousands of years. The collective consciousness on earth has been so toxic and challenging for so long that any soul who graduates has achieved a huge advancement in their eternal learning journey. Earth is not our 'real home' we are here on assignment, secondment, away for school and the average 70 years or so we are here is a blip in time although when you are here I know it can feel like eternity.

Our true home is in another dimension, in all religions the concept of afterlife is present and the idea in these religions is that you live a good life, you get to go the afterlife that is a utopia where everything is good, loving and nice. That place is our true home where we all come from, and we choose to incarnate into a physical body for the experience and attainment of spiritual advancement through the experiences we plan for ourselves during any particular lifetime.

Before we are born we plan the lessons of our life, what we choose to experience and learn, we choose our parents, partners, children (if we have them), jobs, socioeconomic background, country of birth etc. The plan is quite detailed, we also choose guides who are not incarnated in this particular lifetime to help us along the way and keep us on track. The caveats? When we are born we forget where our true home is, why we are here and what the plan was! The reason for this is to heighten the advancement experience. Secondly we have free will to choose what we want, and this can be and is often not in line with what we planned.

It is important to note that linear time only exists on the earth plane, outside of the earth dimension everything is NOW, the past, present and future as we see it is NOW. It is hard to get your head around but understanding that when you plan your life you see the possible futures that your life will take place in, it is like having a birdseye view of your life.

So many of us go through our lives making mistakes, getting into patterns of behaviour, feeling like we need to control everything and often feeling totally out of control of our lives and don't really understand the reasons why. Part of it is because our society does not teach us how to connect to our spiritual self, particularly in the western world. Our guides in spirit help us to remember our mission and our life lessons, they also help by creating synchronicities where we meet the right person (or wrong one depending on our planned lessons) at the time we are meant to. The key thing to remember is that if we learn our lesson we move on in our lives to the next experience and lesson we set ourselves. If we don't learn our lesson then those lessons repeat themselves. An example, we set ourselves a lesson that we were going to experience a relationship where our partner does not treat us well, say emotional abuse and controlling behaviour. Our lesson is to have enough self-esteem that we do not accept the poor behaviour and the way we are treated and we no longer continue the relationship. This sounds simple but anyone who has been in this situation will know that it is far more complicated and challenging to deal with and to walk away from. We may end this relationship however

25

the core lesson was to have more self-esteem, and we will be challenged again by bringing another person who is controlling and abusive into our lives, if we choose not to get involved with them because we read the signs and have good self-esteem, bingo, lesson learned. However if we get involved again with this new person the cycle will continue until or if we learn the lesson.

Death, Grief, and Loss

Death is the natural cycle of life and every single one of us will experience the death of someone we love. Grieving is the natural order of things and allowing this process to happen is vital to our future emotional, mental and physical health. People often find it easier to accept the loss of an older person. You will hear people saying things like 'they had a good life, lived to a good age' for example. However if a younger person dies it is often seen as more of a tragedy, 'they had no chance to live a full life, it shouldn't have happened to them' are examples of things people say. People will also often look at 'good and bad people" criminals v's good citizens and if the 'good person or good citizen" dies then this is also considered more of a tragedy. Murder or disappearances of people are particularly challenging to deal with.

By recognising the following it can help with the process of grief and accepting the loss of a loved one:

- The physical separation from the person who has passed is only temporary and you will be reunited with that person when it is the end of your current incarnation.
- Each person sets exit points in their life as part of their life plan and these points are opportunities when they can leave their current incarnation if they

have fulfilled their life plan or if they do not want to continue with the life lessons.

- Some people plan for their lives to be short and their primary mission is to teach the people around them through their struggles, sacrifice, disability, or illness. Children who are born disabled or die young are good examples of this.
- The grief and loss of a loved one is part of your own life lesson and to fully embrace the emotions and then let them go is part of the way to move forward with your own path; this could also include you letting go of any co-dependency you had with the person who died.
- The person who has passed is once again home and free from any pain they suffered, free to live their life as before and will be happy and content. Their greatest wish for you, the person left behind is for you to get on with your life, learn your lessons and then go home to them. Matters of money, where they are buried, and all earthly issues do not matter to them at all.

Health

The current medical system has some amazing carers and dedicated practitioners who really want to do their best for their patients, however the system in which they work is really quite flawed. Having a very personal experience of battling the system to get the right care, and indeed the answers to a wide number of issues that my wife experienced over a number of years has given me a particular insight. These are some of my observations:

- In many cases symptoms are treated and the root cause not investigated or discovered.

- The answer to treat most conditions or illnesses is prescription drugs, one only has to observe a GP surgery in the UK to see how many patients come out from seeing the doctor with a prescription in hand.
- There are a number of side effects and, or contraindications that prescription drugs have. You have medication for one thing and the side effects causes something else that you then have further medication for.
- Many drugs only marginally improve situations and often the body can become dependent on them.
- I challenge you to investigate the manufacturers of pharmaceutical products and see who they are and how big these corporations are and indeed how much money they make. They do a great job of promoting what they are doing to create cures and improve people's lives but think about this - Pharmaceutical companies are in business to make money, sick people who use their drugs and keep needing them are lifelong customers and they (the companies) make a lot of money, so is it in the pharmaceutical companies' interests to cure people without need for life-long use?
- The current medical system has no allowance or consideration for anything other than science based on physics, biology and chemistry. They have only just scratched the surface of how the mind impacts the body. The medical system would not even consider the influence of the spirit and any other related metaphysical teachings despite there being more and more evidence to support the fact that natural and holistic treatments are very effective.

Any form of medical treatment in itself does not heal. In reality, surgery, drugs, and various other methods of medical treatment attempt to set a stage in the body, wherein the Natural Healing Forces, Laws of Nature, or God can more effectively and readily heal the body. Medical doctors actually set the stage for healing. In other words, they cooperate in the healing process, but do not themselves heal. The operative laws of nature contained within Universal Consciousness do the actual healing. (Dr Paul Masters 2016)

To be healed no matter what method is used, one has to prepare and pave the way for healing to occur through raised consciousness, positive affirmations and thought processes, and letting go of negativity. I have read or heard about stories where someone has been told they are going to die and within a very short space of time they do. Or when someone is told they are going to die and have such strong motivation and determination through a positive attitude that they either recover or live a lot longer than projections by doctors. There are some key factors in play that go further in explaining whether or not someone survives a serious illness. As well as a positive mindset other factors include, the choice of an exit point to leave the current incarnation and to use the illness as a learning situation and to become stronger in mind, body, and spirit. Ultimately each individual decides for themselves, their true self (spirit or soul) is the one who is in control. This sheds light on why some people heal and others do not, why 'miracles' seem to happen with some and not others. It also means that YOU now have a choice; you can take your own healing into your own hands and choose the best method or methods for you to be able to heal.

The process of life evaluation, lesson learning, positivity, higher consciousness and so on is what sets the stage and an environment for self-healing to occur. Connection to ones true-self and spirit consciousness (soul) allows the energy of healing to work with the chosen method, whether it be traditional medical, natural alternative or ancient healing. I prefer natural healing methods because they are more in rhythm with nature and Mother Earth and are more synergistic with our physiology. I would rather use crystals, herbs, good food and essential oils to heal than chemically produced manmade drugs. I am not in any way belittling the work that scientific medical researchers do, the ones whose hearts are genuinely about trying to help cure people. However I feel that the natural way is the better way.

Religion

Religious beliefs have influenced our society and people's behaviour for a long time. There are some positive influences such as moral behaviour guidelines however the various churches and places of worship in the main have instilled beliefs that would separate us from God rather than have us believe that we are a part of God as per metaphysical teachings. There are many names for God consciousness given by mainstream religion, or alternative religions, none of the names matter, you call God consciousness whatever feels right for you. You may simply refer to God consciousness as The Universe. The other key thing about most religions is that they tell you what to think and how you should feel and act. This does not allow for your true self to bring forth your own truth and adds to creating a society of people who struggle to really think for themselves.

I always found it very contradictory that the Christian bible teaches of a vengeful, angry judgemental God and a God that one has to earn love from, this viewpoint just did not seem to be right. Surely God gives unconditional love no matter what? Religion has also told people who they can and cannot love. I also found it hard to come to terms with organisations who do not see women as equal when it comes to being close to God; in the UK, woman were only allowed to become bishops in the Church of England in 2014, despite extensive equality legislation coming into force in 2010. One has to question how this can be right, as many other faiths also have separated women and have all sorts of reasons why to justify it. The purpose discussing this is to give you an opening, if you have been brought up with a particular faith did you ever question the doctrine? Did it somehow not sit right with you? Perhaps you have not had a faith because you saw and felt the contradictions? Whatever your situation, search deep into your intuition about what is your truth regarding your faith or lack of it.

One does not need to follow any particular faith or teaching to believe in God consciousness. It is this consciousness that links us together, binds us, unifies us and connects us to the earth we share with its beautiful creatures, the stars and planets in the sky and the wider universe we are not yet consciously aware of.

Life on other Planets

It is interesting how science has a very limited view of how to prove that life exists on other planets. Additionally the use of 'science fiction' to almost ridicule the idea that other life forms exist in the universe or to make aliens look bad and western humans look good has been commonly used by media, film and TV. You may have felt deep inside that you believe in the existence of extraterrestrial life even though you did not have proof. Part of finding your way to your true self is coming to an understanding with yourself that you are deeply connected to the universe and all living beings within it, and that includes not only life on earth but life in the rest of the universe as well, no matter what form or forms they may take. Have an open heart so that you can come to a truth about who you are as a human being and where you come from; the more that you awaken and begin your journey of discovery the more you will come to a strong realisation that your previous understanding about the world was very limited.

Male & Female Roles

For centuries we have lived in a world where men have dominated and until fairly recent times women were not permitted into many areas of work. It is also an observation that women who are successful in the world often have to use a lot of masculine energy in order to be successful. This subjugation of woman over the centuries has been hugely detrimental to the world. The domination of wounded masculine energy and suppressed divine feminine energy created some of the darkest times that this world has ever experienced and we are still in the dying phases of those dark times. Up until the 1960's in the western world when gender roles started to change a little there had been clear roles of men and women, men were the breadwinners who would go out to work and women would stay at home and be a homemaker and raise the children. In fact obey was in the marriage vows and women were expected to obey their husbands. There was also a clear way in which men and women were expected to behave. Indeed so-called neurosis that included nervousness, anxiety and depression were thought to be the frailty of women and not men by early psychologists. Any deviations from the traditional roles were met with condemnation from families and society causing a great deal of pain and anguish. Women were emotional and men were not allowed to be emotional or they were not considered to be a man.

This way of living and behaviour created a huge wounding to both masculine and feminine and as gender roles began to change a great deal of confusion was created on how each gender was supposed to behave and this led to misery and unhappiness and the unfolding of the old way of life. New found freedom for women, the growing acceptance of other forms of sexuality other than heterosexual, increase in divorce, decrease in marriage and the make up of nontraditional families all contributed to the change in gender roles. Men were now expected to take a full role in parenting and many women said they wanted more sensitive male partners. All these changes as progressive as they are have also caused a number of issues. Women who have been able to let go of some of the wounding still find themselves struggling to gain equality in the world of work, despite legislation for equal pay being in place for decades still there is a huge gap between men and women's pay in some companies and these companies are not prosecuted. The confusing role for men has led to issues with the mental health of an increasing number of men, according to the UK Office for National Statistics out of the total number of suicides in 2018 two thirds were men.

I don't mean to give a history lesson but it is important to understand that the wounding of both feminine and masculine roles is yet to be resolved. I have heard a number of prominent speakers on the rise of the feminine and women talk about women being the future and how this will improve the world. I have no doubt that a lot more women need to be in more prominent positions however it is important to understand the nature of the soul and its role in gender in physical form. The soul or spirit is genderless, and this is because we only take the form of gender when we incarnate. Every one of us is a mix of masculine and feminine energy and the best way in which we function whether male or female or non-binary is to have an EQUAL BALANCE of both masculine and feminine energy. This has nothing to do with sexuality but to do with behaviour and getting the best from life and being healthy mentally, physically and emotionally as well as spiritually.

A divinely awakened man would be the physical embodiment of the masculine and will often take on the role of the masculine traits including confidence, strength, protection, courage, assertiveness, logic, direction, clarity and stability. This would be whilst he is being fully connected to his feminine energy of unconditional love, sensitivity, intuition and kindness for example. A divinely awakened woman is the physical embodiment of the feminine and will often take on the role of the feminine traits including creativity, emotional, tenderness, and nurturing. This would be whilst she is being fully connected to her masculine energy of focus, responsibility, discipline, and power for example. These circumstances however are not the case if there is wounding with the masculine and feminine within and this can lead to a number of emotional and behavioural problems and issues in relationships. Later on in the next section I will discuss examples of this that you can compare yourself to in order to help you identify where you are and what changes you may need to make.

Children & Parents

We are first influenced by our caregivers (parents and people or persons that raise us), their behaviour towards us teaches us about how we should or should not behave. We often see people either being exactly like a parent or making sure that they are exactly not like a parent. We also see people take on the likes and dislikes of parents such the type of food they like or don't like. Parents often have a fixed idea about how their child should be or what they should do. I have heard about parents who spend hours taking their child from one club, class and activity to another over a weekend. Wanting to make sure that they do not miss out on anything, exhausting schedules of stuff that is often not liked or really wanted by the child. They do it because they want to please the parent or because they want to fit in with their friends who do the same activities. What is often forgotten is that parenting is a two-way street and requires a fine balance. Parents need to allow their children to guide them to what they want, spending time truly listening to them or understanding their behaviour (even what looks like poor behaviour) and then responding accordingly. Openness to new ideas and possibilities is really important and remember our children teach us too! Later on I discuss the inner child and how to use this knowledge to better parent your children.

Education

A set curriculum is becoming far too limiting for many young people today, methods of teaching and learning are not fluid enough in many circumstances and individual needs are challenging for teachers to meet. Don't get me wrong. From my experience of teaching its a very hard job to be fully inclusive in lessons, to make lessons that are dynamic and engaging week in, week out, teachers simply do not have enough time to do that in most circumstances in schools. The emergence or now recognition of a number of so-called learning difficulties is highlighting these issues. In reality it is my belief that many of the these so-called learning difficulties are not difficulties at all, the child is merely seeing the world in a different way or has a different way of learning to others, that is their own unique way of learning and not a "difficulty' at all.

Outdated curriculum is no longer preparing young people for the world including the omission of huge parts of human history. Things that are sorely lacking in education is how to take care of the mind, body, and spirit, how to have a good relationship with yourself and then with others. The pressure on children to pass exams, cope with changes in their bodies as they grow, cope with the adults and other children in their lives and how their behaviour affects them is huge and not to be underestimated. Competition and the feeling that children have to be a certain way to be successful in life brings about a loss of innocence and the wonder of all things new, making them grow up too soon. All this pressure in early life sets the roots and foundations for a lack of self-worth as they grow and age.

For people of all ages there seems to be a lack of teaching of critical thinking, information is taken on face value, a balanced two-sided approach is often lacking. Few people seem to ask important questions like why, what, who, is this valid, where does the information come from, who collated it, are they associated with a big company who might pay them to give the results etc…. It should not be underestimated the influence that the media and social media have on how information is presented to the public and the motives behind the news articles that are being reported. I am saying here, open your eyes, question, look at the opposing argument, ask where the so-called facts are coming from etc

Further and Higher Education

I worked in further and higher education establishments in the UK, in Further Education it was clear that compulsory education had failed a lot of students, I refer to the system and not the dedicated teachers who work within it. I witnessed some great further education teachers who enriched the learning experience for many students. However much like their compulsory education colleagues they were overworked and underpaid due to a massive lack of funding from government. Trying to prepare young people for higher education, the world of work and coping with their lives is a challenge for all working in further education.

My observations were that in higher education there often seemed to be an imbalance between quality of teaching and support for students, and focus on research. Although it is right that students at this level take responsibility for their own learning there was often a sink or swim mentality. Many of the degree programmes focus on theoretical concepts that without practical application many find hard to grasp. Research in universities are often funded by large businesses and corporations who have their own interests in what comes out of the research being undertaken and this is then passed onto the students and back out into the world of work. Now this could be a good thing because it prepares students for the reality of work and enables them with the latest research concepts. Some students who are naturally critical thinkers and great creators thrive and add value to the work place however when you dig deep here you see that for many students this does not help them in a practical way and many students come away from degree programmes and do not use the knowledge that they gained from their study in their everyday working or personal lives.

My idea of how education should be may be to some utopian in nature however I feel that children are our future. We should be doing everything we can to teach them how to be fully rounded individuals who love themselves, love others, have a sense of community, how to be tolerant of the differences between people and to celebrate the similarities. For children to take a path in life that suits their skills and abilities and their hearts' desires. We need to start somewhere in creating change for our world and teaching children many of the concepts in this book would be a great place to start in achieving this.

Sex & Sexuality

For hundreds of years we have been indoctrinated by mainstream religions that only heterosexual expression of our sexuality is the right one and that any deviation from that is wrong and against God. In nature we see male and female coming together for the purpose of procreation however humans are on earth for a range of different reasons. Procreation can be and is for many an important part of why we are here and certainly our physical biology requires male and female to create new life; but many are now choosing not to have children whatever their sexual preference. However if you bring forth the concepts I have discussed regarding reincarnation and life planning it brings sexuality into a different light. There are a number of reasons for different sexual expressions; as we incarnate into different lives we do so as different genders, male in this life, female in the previous one for example, this is so we can fully experience what it is like to be both man and woman.

- We carry cell memory when we incarnate and this is brought forth into a new life when we are born. If we were female in our previous life and are now male, the cells may remember what it is like to be female and that can cause sexual attraction towards men instead of woman or in addition to being attracted to women.
- We may choose to experience what it is like to be in a relationship with someone of the same gender as a life experience to teach us that our soul is androgynous and that gender does not matter only love does. Additionally we have the experience of prejudice, discrimination and the like that many gay people experience in life.
- Transgender can be caused by either of the above scenarios and is a particularly challenging life situation and brave souls undertake this life theme.
- Choice is another factor, if a woman has been deeply wounded by a man and finds it impossible to trust in a man again she may choose to receive love from another woman. I know of some examples personally where people have chosen a same sex relationship because of abuse.

Key message here, it does not matter what your sexual expression (orientation) is, you are here to experience and to love, NO ONE including God, the Creator, Source or whoever you choose to call God will JUDGE YOU. Whatever any other human being thinks about you is not your concern, only what you think about yourself matters. What should be understood is that during love making energy is exchanged between the two people and casual encounters that are for gratification and not love can bring about the exchange of unwanted negative energies in addition to the risks to health if safe sex is not adhered to. This energy can be extremely negative and can have a big impact to the health of the energetic body, as well as affecting emotions and negative mind talk.

There is also a lot of misunderstanding about our sexual selves and the role in which sex plays in our lives. Whatever your physical gender most people struggle to understand and know the sexual part of themselves let alone that of another person. When you are having a spiritual awakening it is important to begin to recognise that there is a link between finding your true self (your spiritual self or soul) and your sexual self. As discussed earlier everything is energy and sexual energy is extremely powerful and understanding and harnessing your sexual energy is really important for your mind, body, and spirit balance. Sexual energy is the source and power of our divine selves and if that energy is harnessed it is extremely healing and can support excellent health even in later life and indeed longevity of life. The Tao teachings on the harnessing of sexual energy are a good place to begin in learning how to do this for yourself. Mantak Chia is a prolific writer and teacher and I highly recommend reading his books and using the methods that he teaches.

FEAR - False Evidence Appearing Real

False evidence appearing real, this is such an accurate definition of fear! We all feel fear at one time or another but as an emotion it was only meant to keep us from real harm and not causing us to damage our well being in such a profound way. Fear is the top inhibitor to a happy life, it is led by the ego and as an emotion is extremely corrosive to the human body. Fear is what prevents you from enjoying the wonders of life and to appreciate all that is beautiful in this world. What are some of the most common fears?

- Success - More than the fear of failure, the fear of success is much stronger so much so that people will sabotage their own success. Why? It is deeply connected to a lack of self-worth, people do not feel worthy of the success. The ego takes fear into hyperdrive when success comes or is near, a whole host of what if's are laid out to edge you toward running away, worst case scenarios run riot in the mind and all of this takes you away from success and holds you back.
- Failure - Failure is feared because of judgement. Being judged by others based on societal guidelines, are you married or in a successful relationship, have children, great career, lots of money, big house, good education etc. If you don't have these things then you will be judged as not being successful or being a failure. Self-judgement is even more powerful, all of the worst things you feel about yourself surface and you end up fulfilling your own prophecy about yourself by failing.
- Loneliness - A lack of self-love and connection to your true self brings forth a fear of being alone. We feel that we need other people to fulfil us, we often search for other people as life partners or friends to

make us feel good. Imagine not 'needing' others to feel good, imagine feeling good without them AND then having those people in your life as a beautiful extra, then you would feel amazing.

- Rejection, abandonment, betrayal - Fear of rejection often prevents us from doing things, asking someone out for example or applying for a job or starting studying. Fear of rejection can come from an experience when you were rejected in the past or as a result of poor self-esteem. Fear of betrayal, again this can be there because of a past betrayal or a lack of trust in others caused by other people's behaviour towards you. Fear of abandonment can go very deeply and manifest in different behaviours particularly those defined as wounded feminine (present within both genders - see page 76). Abandonment can also be linked to a wounded inner child as a result of being abandoned in childhood.
- Illness and ageing - Fear of illness is quite common, this fear often leads to actually manifesting illness in life. Fear of ageing forces a range of behaviours including:
- Mid-life crisis including extra relationship affairs, new careers, new hobbies, dressing younger and more....
- Denial or failure to get medical assistance for ailments
- Apathy about life, the present and possible future
- Hypochondria
- Death - Fear of death stems from a lack of faith in the eternity of your spirit, guilt about your behaviour in this lifetime and indoctrination by religion that would lead us to falsely believe in the concept of hell and a wrathful, judgement God that will not allow us into heaven if we have sinned and not atoned for those sins. None of which are true. (see page 30 for comments about this)

Abuse

Abuse happens all around us, to children, between partners, to animals, in work places, schools, colleges and universities. It is a sad fact that everything from physical and sexual abuse to bullying, harassment, and emotional and mental abuse is prevalent in today's society. It is my belief that abuse is a symptom of the society which has been created. This has been done with a wounded masculine dominated world, the lack of divine feminine energy in the world has brought about poor levels of income. A huge gap between rich and poor, a lack of education in self-care, self-love, having successful relationships, parenting; poor diets full of processed sugar, artificial ingredients and GMO's. A system of religion that is masculine dominated and teaches separation from God (the universe etc), and also teaches prejudice against other faiths, sexuality and so on; a lack of unity that isolates people from their families and the community around them, shame attached to sufferers of mental health problems and victims of abuse that leads to them not getting help or becoming abusers themselves. Society has created a generation of busy people who never stop, they work, work, work, try to fit in with what is expected of them, escape into movies, gaming, TV and social media, a society that puts immense pressure on its children to perform and do well so they too can thrive in a rat race of materialistic, judgmental competition. Just being a part of this society you are suffering from a type of abuse.

It is hard enough for women to admit to and report being abused because of the dishonour and lack of support that is in place, although there are some good organisations that do a lot to support abuse victims. For men who are abused it is even more difficult because of the stigma attached. According to statistics on the website mankind. org in the domestic abuse category a ratio of two women to one man is abused in the UK however a man who is a victim of abuse is 49% less likely to report it compared to 19% of women and overwhelmingly the perpetrators of abuse against men are women. The website also states that a man is less likely to be believed when accusing a female of abuse and it is common for female perpetrators to turn tables and say that the man is the abuser. Abuse is not gender exclusive in any way and whatever your situation or gender if you are a victim of abuse then you should report it and get help to get yourself out of the situation as safely as possible.

Legislation in the UK defines abuse under the following categories, psychological, physical, sexual, financial and emotional. There are some good websites that you can look at that explain a range of abuse under those categories if you feel that you are a victim of abuse or have been in the past you could check out in the UK or similar organisations in your country:

Mankind - www.mankind.org.uk

Women's Aid - www.womensaid.org.uk

When you are going through an awakening journey it is important to recognise what abuse you have suffered in your life and to be honest if you have been the perpetrator of abuse as well. Unravelling serious abuse should be done with the help of a professional. Along with their help trusting your intuition is really important as it will guide you to how and when to start healing the emotional and psychological scars of abuse. Recognising when those scars of abuse are affecting your life NOW, whether it be in your reactions or reluctance to engage with others or in the building of new relationships as examples is very important.

My own recovery from abuse is ongoing, it's a journey remember!

It started with the recognition that I was actually a victim of abuse and then the types of abuse that I had suffered, realising that I was not alone, that many others suffered the same types of abuse was also important to me. My true self led me through conversations with my mentors, information in my dreams, through personal reflection, journaling and in meditation to understand what had happened to me, why it had happened and how it affected my behaviour and future decision making. It helped me to unlock my subconscious mind and bring forth events and situations that had happened in the past, this was all done a little at a time and only enough for my conscious mind and emotional body to cope with. As more and more pieces unravelled I was then able to see the links between events and decisions I had made, was able to see the root cause of what had happened. Taking responsibility for myself was a vital step in moving away from victimhood. This did not mean that I was responsible for the abuse that happened to me but perhaps in some situations how I enabled it to happen because of my lack of self-esteem. Forgiving myself for allowing abuse to occur was the next step, it was amazing how I blamed myself for a lot of what happened to me. I worked a lot with my inner child (see later in the book) and began to understand how he had been wounded and how I now needed to take care of that part of my consciousness and be very mindful of ensuring that I spent time with the child within me. One of the things that I recognised early on was that I had cut off my ability to really feel anything, I had become so numb inside, not able to feel love, my ego had done a great job of protecting me but the cost was great, my beloved cats help me with this, they are such wonderful teachers of unconditional love. As I was and still am with a person who abused me I had to learn how to shift the power in the relationship and to set boundaries on what behaviour was acceptable or not. This is challenging and does not always work but I kept doing it and bit by bit it improved, there are still relapses but it is much better than it was before. My situation is not ideal and I would always recommend leaving a person who abuses you but I know that this is not always possible so preventing future abuse is very important.

Changing my behaviour, was the key to preventing further abuse happening to me but this had to be done in a positive way, running from life and hiding from people does not help one heal it just covers it up. Being brave and facing how the abuse affected the way I thought, felt, and acted and how I emotionally connected to the world was one of the most challenging parts of my recovery. The self-enquiry led me to a much deeper understanding of how abuse had affected how I saw myself, how others viewed me, and how the abuse had affected my ability to feel alive and whole. As I began to heal the wounds of abuse I started to open my heart and feel emotions that had been squashed and hidden for so long, this was a frightening experience and I had to wrestle with my ego to keep my heart open and allow the pain to surface and come out. The crying helped, as did the invocation of my spiritual guides, journalling about my feelings and sharing with my mentors and trusted friends. All of the exercises and tools in this book I have used to help me with my recovery. Giving myself compassion particularly during bad days when I felt I was not making any progress at all was also really important.

The other thing that I discovered was that there were layers upon layers of wounding that I had to heal, as one was released another would present itself and this sometimes felt daunting and overwhelming and at these times self-care was immensely important. Positively with each layer that was released and healed more room was created within me to bring more love, joy, happiness, trust and wisdom into my life. This made me stronger and more able to cope with the next level of healing that I needed to do. I am still on this journey and am confident with each layer of healing that I will once again feel fully whole and alive again and thank my true self for showing me the way.

Abundance / Law of Attraction

Abundance is an interesting word. What thoughts, feelings and images come up for you when you read the word? Many people associate abundance with money and financial plenty, for me and many others it means so much more than that. Abundance simply defined is a lot of something; so if we translate this to our lives then it means, a lot of money, a lot of health, a lot of love, a lot of freedom, a lot of peace and so on. So why are some people abundant and some people not? This is all about how you view abundance and you're entitlement to it.

Let's discuss financial abundance, some of you have deep-seated beliefs about money, in many world religions there is a view that having lots of money is sinful, very often people think that they want and deserve money but do not do what is needed to attract it to them. One of the biggest mistakes that people make (and this is as a result of the type of economic world we live in) is to put values on everything, this is worth this much, this is worth that much, I paid this much for that, I worked hard to pay for this or that and so on.

Attracting abundance into your life is a process, many of the exercises, activities and meditations in this book are designed to bring you abundance in every form. There are lots of self-help books that guide you on how to attract great things into your life and a lot of them have some great ideas and processes.

For me however the core element of attracting abundance into your life is to create a mind, body, and spirit balance, to find your true self through self-enquiry and the discovery that you are a divine being who has the right to abundance in all areas of your life. There are no half measures, no settling for, no 'I don't deserve', no I don't have enough education or I don't know the right people or I need money to make money. None of these excuses are relevant, work on yourself, embody your true self, create a mind, body, and spirit balance and all the abundance in the world will come to you. I know it sounds simple and it is, making those changes are challenging but even working towards that is going to help you to bring more abundance into your life. I cannot say this enough, you create your own life through your thoughts and emotions and how you project them into your reality, if you believe that you deserve abundance then it will come to you, if you send out positive thoughts and emotions regarding success and abundance, then it will come to you. If you struggle with abundance in your life then you need to evaluate what is holding you back, is it fear of success? Do you believe that you are not worthy of money or love in your life? Is there trauma that you need to heal to bring you into better health? This requires some deep inner enquiry to establish what it is that you need to do in order to improve the abundance in your life. There may be deep-seated beliefs that you are harbouring regarding money, love or health. Using the 7 Pillars of Personal Change in the next section to help with this. Becoming aware of your internal critic and the inner dialogue that you are having with yourself is also very important. What negative things are you saying to yourself that is preventing abundance coming into your life?

YOUR AWAKENING JOURNEY

The Seven Pillars of Personal Change

These 7 Pillars or stages are cyclical in nature, each one follows the other and one can then go back to the beginning to go deeper or start something anew. Many people get to Pillar 6 and then go back to the beginning if the new ways they are testing did not work out, which can happen sometimes. The content in this book is designed to help you particularly with the first four Pillars and then 5 through 7 is up to you to decide if you want to change, what you want to change and how, testing new ways and then adopting them permanently.

1. RAISING AWARENESS
2. OBSERVATION
3. MAKING SENSE
4. CHALLENGING BELIEFS
5. DECIDING ON CHANGE
6. TESTING NEW WAYS
7. ADOPTING NEW WAYS

These seven pillars or stages I use whenever I am making a change in my personal behaviour, the amount of time spent at each stage varies according to what is being changed, how ingrained the behaviour is and whether behaviours are linked to other habits or patterns. It is extremely common for people to start on a self-improvement programme and then to lose heart and not complete it. Or for the change to be temporary and to go back to old patterns of behaviour.

Change is not easy for many people, we offer a great deal of resistance and this is because we become comfortable with how things are, our ego feels safe and secure and convincing it that change is a good idea can be half the battle! Embedding lasting changes to your behaviour in your daily life requires a deep commitment to self-improvement and motivation to see it through when things get tough.

Lets me be very clear again, that with any self-improvement programme you will fall off the wagon, have a day where you did not do what you planned to, went back to an old habit, thought you were doing great and then have a period of time where you feel low and as if you have not made any improvements at all, this is all NORMAL! What I found was that when I would dip and have a bad time I would somehow forget everything that I had learnt, all the tools I had at my disposal to help me get back on the wagon and improve how I was feeling, it often took a friend to say to me, have you done XYZ to help, crazy but true. The 7 Pillars of Personal Change can help you with this simply go back to Pillar 1 and raise your awareness of how and why you have fallen off the wagon or are having a hard time and go through the stages to help you get back on track. You have all of the resources and tools to help you to create a fantastic life for yourself, the answers actually come from within you and using the 7 Pillars and working on many of the suggestions, ideas, exercises and meditations in this book will help you do just that.

Raising awareness

This stage is about raising your awareness of self :

- Take regular breaks throughout the day
- Look at your phone for just a short time then put it away during the breaks. If you can take a walk outside connect to nature and really use all 5 senses to experience where you are; if you can't go outside find somewhere quiet and just sit.
- Allow thoughts to come, what are they about? The past? The future? Try not to judge the thoughts just allow them to come and go (this means not allowing one thought to lead to another about that subject, not being self-critical, or critical of others)
- Allow emotions and feelings to surface again notice them, without judgment. What they are? Where you feel them in your body? Then let them go
- If you find your mind is trying to tell you things you need to do then make a list of them
- If there is a bigger issue in your life that this exercise raises then recognise that it is something that you will need to spend more time on later
- Start to observe and be aware of how your life is in reality, potential things that you may like to change, try to get a true picture of how your life really is.

Observation

During this stage you need not be concerned with analysing just try to observe

- Using your new awareness start to observe what your thoughts are during daily activities
- Start to observe what your emotions and feelings are during daily activities, and where you feel them in your body

- Observe how you interact with other people; do certain people trigger thoughts or feelings and emotions to come, again if they do practice not judging them just go with it. (note that you should mentally separate people in different parts of your life to make the "making sense" section easier)
- Observe how you interact with any pets
- Observe your thoughts, feelings and emotions during any leisure activities and note them
- You may want to journal about your observations or just make a list

Making Sense

This is all about making sense of the observations, what does it mean, what impact is it having on life, love, relationships, career, money and so on

Take each area of your life love, friends, career, leisure, spiritual etc. and do the following:

- What thoughts, feelings and emotions do you have about a particular area of your life?
- What do those thoughts, feelings and emotions mean for you?
- What impact are those thoughts, feelings and emotions having on that particular part of your life?
- Write down or journal what you have learned from this activity

Challenging Beliefs

This is the process of starting to challenge yourself, challenge who you are, what you want, what you believe and why and whether the things you believe and do are serving you or not. The previous steps will have raised a number of issues that you can challenge yourself on some examples include:

- A limiting belief that you are not good enough for a successful career
- A belief that you have to prove to your family or boss that you are successful and good at what you do
- A limiting belief that you have to be a super parent to prove to society that you are a good parent
- The limiting belief that you don't have it in you.
- The limiting belief that others are better than you, giving you the feeling that you must step aside and let them pass you by.
- The limiting belief that you don't have sufficient abilities.
- The limiting belief that because you have failed in the past, you probably would fail again in the future.

And so on…….

During this process do not listen to the ego state of the mind, trust your intuition, your feelings, this is a chance to really get to grips with what you truly want and what is holding you back.

Deciding on Change

This is where you use the information gained by challenging your beliefs to decide that you what you want to change and why. This is a vital stage as the decision to change must be made both consciously and subconsciously in order to be open to new ways. Then decide what change will be made, and do not try too much all at once, deicide on the thing or things that will have the most impact initially. Don't overcomplicate it, make the changes simple for you to achieve particularly at the beginning of your journey.

Examples could be:

- I will take all of my breaks at work and will spend at least 15 minutes being mindful

- I will make time to spend time on something I want to do
- I use the breathing exercises when I am feeling stressed

Testing New Ways

This is about trying and testing what changes have been decided, remember that changing behaviour is not easy and you should not get disheartened if at first you do not succeed or if you fall off the wagon temporarily, all you do is go back to the earlier stages and start the process over, this could be observing why you did not succeed and then deciding to try a different way or approach.

Adopting New Ways

This is when you have tested new ways and seen changes and where you start to integrate them into your daily life and they become the new normal for you. Once this is achieved you can then go through the stages again and work on something else.

Mindfulness

There is a lot of attention being given to mindfulness at the moment, I am seeing it everywhere, in magazines, colouring books, and health media. If I am seeing it then so must you be, however what is all the hype about? It frustrates me sometimes when something becomes the new big and 'in' thing to do because often the hype then detracts from the core teaching, reasons and benefits. Often people see something and also jump to conclusions or judge what it is without actually properly researching and understanding it. Mindfulness is spoken about a lot in many spiritual and some mainstream media and is suggested that it is a useful tool to reduce stress, improve mental health and increase happiness. Mindfulness is not a thing that you sometimes do, like yoga or even meditation, it is a way of life. Mindfulness is the practice of actively taking notice of the present moment.

I refer to mindfulness quite often throughout the book either by name or within a process or exercise. Mindfulness is a state of awareness that you can enter, use, be in, that will help you to become more aware of yourself and others. This awareness then leads you to being able to make personal changes that can improve your life and bring you a much greater peace, calmness, happiness, joy, and love.

Mindfulness is an explanation of something that most of you will do at least some of the time, it is where the mind focuses on one thing and by doing so allows the brain to come off automatic and allows you to be immersed in whatever you are doing rather than thinking about issues, problems, past, future and so on. TV, exercise, craft work and reading are some examples of activities where some people use mindfulness. Mindfulness is when you have full awareness of what you are doing, thinking, and feeling, it allows you to just be in that moment. Behind the hype it is a simple but deeply effective way of being that will really help you. A way of being, not something you put on a list and do alongside your other to do's.

Mindfulness is about being more aware of what is going on around you, when on autopilot you can miss so many things that are happening and being more present in each moment can help you to be much more effective at daily tasks. It can also bring a better sense of calm and peace when doing even the simplest of activities, it can really help with active listening and preventing miscommunication with others.

Autopilot is the state when we really are focussed on doing and it can be useful sometimes but if you really try hard to be more consciously aware of what you are doing when doing a task you will find that you are less likely to make mistakes and you will also appreciate even the simplicity of a task for example. A lot of people struggle to stop doing and just be, they feel they should be doing something rather than just sitting and being with themselves. Sometimes that is because they then begin to think and feel things that they have suppressed and this feels uncomfortable so they just hide away. If this is you then you may find that stopping is hard and the thoughts and emotions that come up are difficult. There are some ways to overcome this including, writing them down on a list or journalling about them, spending dedicated time daily to write down worries or concerns. Remember not to judge yourself regarding any thoughts or feelings you have, try to remain an objective observer. I will also reiterate that if you have suffered trauma then seeking help from a counsellor or professional therapist is recommended. Most of the exercises in this book have a mindful basis. It should also be noted that for any self-improvement process to work you need to be mindful otherwise you are not going to get the best out of it.

Dealing with Mind Talk

Mindfulness can help you with dealing with mind talk, the more aware you are the more likely you are to be able to understand and do something about it. The conscious mind is very efficient. Its purpose is to create thoughts however a large number of people are addicted to overthinking. The problem with thoughts is that they lead from one thing to another. One minute you are trying to remember if you have fed the cat and the next the cat being fed has led to needing to buy cat food, to going to the supermarket, making a mental list of what else you need, thinking about food menus and so on.

People can also have what they consider to be bad thoughts about themselves or other people and then find that they are judging themselves because of such thoughts and being very negative about themselves. This leads to physiological problems, physical pain or discomfort somewhere in the body. Your thoughts do not define you, the more you programme the mind to think positively the less your mind will create bad thoughts. Using positive affirmations (see the next section) can really help with this.

If you analyse your own mind talk you may also discover that you are saying very negative things to yourself about yourself. The majority of people are very hard on themselves and they are over critical. This internal critic is led by the ego mind who wants to keep you safe and does actually have your best interests in mind however to do this it resorts to negative self-talk to stop you from what it perceives as putting yourself in danger. It creates scenarios of greater and greater disaster in order to protect you from harm and stop you putting yourself in harms way. It will project awful versions of the future and bring up experiences from the past.

Deeper investigation into mind talk can also lead to the discovery of another voice saying negative things to you and no you are not going crazy! If you had a significant event in your past when a parent or teacher for example said something to you this can come back again in the present if a similar situation is triggered. An example could be if you did something wrong as a child and your parent said 'don't do that you stupid girl' this creates an imprint in your mind and you may find that the voice that is telling you that you are stupid is not your voice but that of the parent who said it to you when you were a child. There are a number of ways to deal with overthinking and using the 7 Pillars of Personal Change and raising your awareness of what you mind talk is saying to you is a good place to start. Going on to observe triggers that may lead to excessive overthinking the next stage. Starting to understand and make sense of what you are thinking and what will help you to start to manage your mind in a better way. The brain is a muscle and needs to be trained, taking control of overthinking and going deeper into listening to your intuition will really help. Throughout the process try to resist going into judgement, you need to understand but judgement will simply send you further into poor self-esteem and will feed the internal critic to be even more negative.

Dealing with overthinking and negative thought patterns

Mindfulness is really the key to managing overthinking and using the 7 Pillars of Personal Change process alongside mindfulness practices will help to overcome intrusive mind talk. However when working through what thoughts you are having and the triggers for them can lead to you uncovering deeper pain and hurt that are causing some of the overthinking issues. Any form of trauma that we experience will have an impact on us in one way or another. It can often manifest in dark, negative and self-hating thoughts that can lead to anxiety, depression and other mental health issues. I would always advise obtaining professional help for any of these issues, a counsellor, therapist etc who can support you to deal with PTSD and other similar mental health issues. However doing some or all of the following can help you alongside the support of a professional.

Identifying Patterns & Routines

We all have routines in our lives, things that we do every day, many of them you may not even be aware of, such as always having a cup of tea or coffee when you wake up in the morning, brushing your teeth at a certain time, going grocery shopping on the same day every week, taking the same route to work and so on. Some routines are forced upon us by others. Many of you who have children will have to pick them up at a certain time from school for example, or your work dictates when you must be there. However there are patterns or routines that you could change. The things within your control, what time you eat might be one, if you go to the gym then go at a different time perhaps or simple things like a different TV programme, a new flavour of a food you like, a new dish to cook, changing the time you do something during the day, again you get the picture. Think about how you look forward to a holiday (even if this is just time off from your usual routine), it is a change in pattern and often makes us feel refreshed and renewed.

Why would all of this make any difference? Behaviour patterns in our lives create pathways in our brains. The pathways become stronger the more we do something and that then makes it easier for us to do things. For example learning to drive, many of you who have been driving for years do not consciously think about doing it. These patterns also create energy and if a pattern is old or stagnant then this energy also becomes old and stagnant and can create issues for you in your life and this can lead to both physical and emotional issues.

There may be daily life patterns you cannot necessarily change and they may not feel like 'bad' routines for you, however if you want to start to make changes in your life you need to start by identifying physical patterns and routines in your daily life. Over a period of 7 days consciously observe the patterns or routines in your life. What you are looking for are patterns that you can change if you want to, write them down as you observe them. At the end of the 7 days look at your list and then get a sense of what you would like to change first. This could just be something small just to test to see how it feels, it does not matter, just do what FEELS right for you. Change can be either exciting and or scary. Try not to give into the fear of change as this will create negative energy in your life and will not support the process of change. If you feel fearful, take a deep breath and calm yourself and then move on, but doing what feels right is important, not what you think is right, what you FEEL is right. Experiment with changing some physical routines and patterns over a two week period and observe and be aware of how those changes affect your life and make you feel. If something does not work for you then go back to what you did before and try something else, there WILL be things that you can change that WILL make you feel better!

Here are some more exercises that will help you with identifying trends, patterns and triggers:

Exercise 1

Make a list of any difficult and good experiences you've had over the last few days, include minor irritations as well as major things that annoyed you. Look at the whole breadth of your life from your computer not working properly to people getting on your nerves to completion of a project being praised or complimented. Please list both positive and negative experiences. Here are some examples you could use – Overslept and late for work, lost internet signal, someone pushed in front of you in a queue, you were complimented by your partner or boss. Makes sure that you include positives as well as negatives.

Now look at your list and write down what emotions you felt in each situation, as many as you can identify.

Filtering:

Look at your list, situations or emotions are too difficult for you to deal with at the moment? Filter those out for now. I would like you to acknowledge them now and then put them aside. This acknowledgement will help you to start the process of healing them. You can then come back to them later on when you feel ready to deal with them.

Exercise 2

Now go back to the list in exercise 1 and choose something that bothered you at the time but is no longer an issue for you. Using the visualisation techniques to recreate the situation and experience it again with all of your senses and make note of the emotions you felt at the time.

Once you have completed the visualisation write down what happened during the recreation paying particular attention to your feelings and your reactions. I would like you not to judge the situation just recognise the emotions.

Exercise 3

Read what you have written about the experience and start to analyse it. How would your reaction have been if you had accepted the reality of the situation rather than perhaps overreacting or if you had chosen a different reaction to the situation. Write your refections down.

Exercise 4

Read what you have written in exercise 3 about the experience and start to analyse it, identify what you have learned about your behaviour and write down any areas that you want to address.

Challenging Beliefs

Do you think about what others will think if you wear a particular item of clothing or say something about a particular topic or if you do a particular activity? As a society we are far too concerned with what other people think of us, please don't be. What you think and feel about yourself is the only thing you should be concerned with. What other people think and feel is on them not you. If you don't care what other people think then that is wonderful, and you are on your way to being free from the effects of other people's judgements.

Dr Paul Masters (2016) discusses false beliefs about yourself very well. A pioneer in metaphysics he recognised after years of research with many clients and students that there were core false beliefs that the majority of people held within them either consciously or unconsciously, the following are based on some of his research:

- Many believe that they are not capable of achieving their hopes and dreams.
- Many believe that other people are better than they are and will always be more successful
- Many believe that they do not have sufficient skills and abilities
- Many believe that if they failed in the past they will fail again in the future
- Many believe that if they are successful that they don't deserve it because of something that they did in the past
- Many believe that they are too self-conscious or shy to succeed

There are of course many more but you get the picture.

In my experience, working with staff and students and clients that 99.9% of people have low self-esteem and this manifests in a number of ways which include:

- A lack of motivation to doing something about things that are wrong in their life
- A strong motivation to attain and achieve personal success and or material things as a substitute for self-esteem
- Allowing others to control them, take away their personal power, abuse them

I could go on listing many different limiting beliefs that people have. The best thing to do is to search yourself and identify some of your own limiting beliefs. The following exercise could be helpful in doing that. You may also note that as you go through the different exercises in this book you may find that you identify further limiting or false beliefs that you hold within that you were not aware of before.

Challenging Beliefs Exercise

- Make a list beliefs you have about yourself. Use my examples as a guide and expand them from there (this may take a few days to do).
- Make the list on the left hand side of the page leaving the right hand side free.
- Leave the list for a day or so then go back to it, add anything you feel you have missed.
- Read each belief out loud and ask yourself the question is this true or false?
- It is important that you are totally honest with yourself and do not allow your ego mind to convince you something is true when it is not.

- Guidelines here are, any belief that assumes you know what someone else is thinking or feeling is false. True beliefs are things that you can 100% be sure of.
- You may come across things that you believe are true but cannot prove. Write down those beliefs, and then search your heart, your intuition. What answer are you getting true or false?
- Once you have placed a true or false next to each belief, look at the false ones and reflect on what they are telling you about yourself.
- This exercise will help you when identifying areas for personal change.

Self-Sabotage

A lack of self-worth can also lead to self-sabotage where individuals deliberately ruin situations because they do not believe that they deserve happiness or health or money. There are also situations where people don't think that they can be more successful than their partner or parent and this limiting belief then causes them to sabotage their life.

I have seen where someone who is in a loving relationship will deliberately start an affair, or start arguments because they do not believe they deserve the love they are feeling and or receiving or simply just cannot accept that they are loved and think that they deserve to be alone and without love.

Procrastination is a big self-sabotage tool, putting things off, finding something else to do, creating a problem to deal with, and so on are all ways to avoid dealing with issues or doing what your heart desires.

The previous exercise on false beliefs will also help you to identify where you have been self-sabotaging your life. Often self-sabotage starts with making excuses and those excuses are linked to a false self-belief about yourself. How many times can you remember when you have made an excuse for not doing something? Common self-sabotage excuses include:

- I don't have enough time
- I don't have enough money
- My family or partner needs me
- I'm too old or too young
- It's not really for me, I'm not meant to do it or go there or be that person
- I'm too tired
- I'm too overweight or not fit enough
- I'm too poorly or my health condition prevents me
- I'm just stuck, I guess this is my lot in life
- Changing takes too much effort and I am ok as I am

There are more of course but I am sure you get the idea.

Self-sabotage is embedded in daily behaviours and it will require you to zoom out of your life and reflect and observe using pillars 1-3 of the change model. Here are some examples that may help you with the process :

- Expecting happiness and success to happen to you osmotically without any effort on your part
- Being perfectionistic and thinking that you are only successful if you arrive at your goal or destination
- Expecting other people to change in order for you to get what you want in life
- You do not let yourself have time for yourself and then spend hours flicking through social media, this includes ignoring the signs that you need to rest and take a break

- You do tasks that are not necessary or do the same thing over and over again instead of opting for a simpler way
- You don't do simple planning activities that would save you time and effort
- You allow others to put on you, including taking responsibility for their actions
- You overcomplicate situations allowing your mind to take over instead of listening to your intuition
- You stay in your comfort zone even though you are unhappy because you allow fear of change to hold you back
- If you can't complete a whole task or job you do nothing rather than some of it
- Your cup is half empty and you choose to see the negative side of situations
- You pretend to listen to advise of friends who try to help you paying lip service to them knowing full well you will never do what they are suggesting
- You make assumptions about other people and set unrealistic expectations of others
- You react with your inner child and think that it's okay to behave that way towards others
- You deliberately take on too much work so that you can prove that you do not have enough time, this includes not saying no to other people
- You do the easy jobs first and leave the big more challenging jobs till last
- You do not complain about being overcharged for something or if you get poor service

Codependency

Codependency is a behaviour where one person enables another's addiction or irresponsible ways, or poor health or lack of maturity because of their own lack of self-worth.

A codependent is often reliant on the other person (or persons) for their sense of identity. They require approval, they put others needs before their own and their whole way of thinking and behaviour is centred around another person or substance (in the case of codependents to addicts). These types of codependent relationships can happen with partners, family, friends and work colleagues.

If you have identified a lot with many of the false beliefs and the self-sabotage examples you are probably in some form of codependency. There are various levels of codependency from extreme to mild and if you identify with this then I do not want you to go into guilt and shame if you have allowed this to happen to you. The important thing is to move towards releasing yourself from the codependency.

Commonly codependents think that they need to help, rescue, save, and support others to be happy. They are not able to have a sense of their own self, their wants, needs and desires always function around others and they get lost in the dependency and lose all sense of self. There are a number of behaviours and traits that can be seen in someone who is codependent. You may have just some of them or all they include:

- Lack of self-esteem
- Is always the victim, things always happen to them
- They find trusting others difficult
- Can be controlling
- Tendency towards perfectionism
- See the negative side of things and focus on their mistakes
- Denies the truth of their situation
- Gets bored easily or feels like nothing satisfies them
- Has a strong need for affection and to be accepted by others

- Does not like being on their own or has a fear of abandonment
- Can become intense in relationships
- Becomes easily depressed
- Does not set boundaries and cannot say no and has feelings of guilt if they do say no
- Has lots of inner child wounding which causes emotional outbursts
- Has issues with intimacy
- Has difficulty stopping and relaxing, always needs do be doing something, overworks
- Struggles to express how they really feel despite feeling hurt or angry or backing down in arguments to avoid others judgment or rejection
- Agrees with others and will compromise personal beliefs, thoughts or feelings to avoid confrontation, disagreement or rejection
- Represses own emotions
- Can be judgemental of others
- Can play power and play control games with others
- Doing things for others that they are capable of doing themselves
- Takes on other people's problems often absorbing their emotions and negative energy
- Does not like change
- Focuses on past hurt and trauma reliving the situation over and over
- Needs to be needed
- Conditions attached to love

Commonly identifying with being codependent can bring a sense of shame that you allowed yourself to become involved in such relationships and whilst that is normal to begin with moving past that feeling towards a plan of how to find your own identity and recover from the codependency is important. If you have been in an abusive situation or feel that you cannot find a way to start to recover from codependency then I advise you to seek out a professional counsellor who can help you.

You will have used Pillars 1 and 2 of the Pillars of Personal Change to identity your own codependent behaviours and traits, this is a huge step in itself. Many codependents are on a river cruise down the long Egyptian river - de-Nile (Denial) and being honest with yourself about your own behaviour without going into victim mode and taking responsibility for yourself is important.

Next, you need to use Pillar 3 and make sense of why this has happened, what the triggers are and how you became codependent. Talking to your mentor or friend who is helping you on this journey is a good idea. This part of the process may require you to look back at your childhood and the relationships you had with caregivers and connect with your inner child, using the guided meditation on page 136 to help you with this. Don't worry if you don't get a complete picture of the cause of codependency straight away it will come as you work your way through. I suggest that you write down the areas in which you have identified you have an issue; you may find commonalities with other areas such has false beliefs, self-sabotage and wounded masculine and feminine traits so group all of the common behaviours and traits you identify in yourself together. Then use Pillars 4 - 7 to decide on what you need to change, remembering not to work on too much at a time. An example roadmap to recovery from codependency could look like :

- Accept that you are codependent, there are layers to this and often denial runs deep
- Seek out therapy if you feel you need it
- Identify what areas you need to recover from, and how you will make those behavioural changes

- Identify how you became codependent including inner child work
- Address any other addictions you may have
- Start the journey to discover who you really are, after a time of codependency you need to find out what you like and don't like, what you really want to do with your life, who you want to be and get to know yourself again. Spending time alone and going out and doing fun things can really help with this stage
- Start the process of differentiating between codependency and attachment, an example could be a caregiver who was codependent can separate the codependency from actual care giving responsibility
- Expect resistance from your ego who is trying to keep you safe and from the person or persons that you were codependent to
- Face the resistance with alternative strategies, playing with the strategies until you find ones that really work for you, this could include trying behaviour that is opposite to codependency
- Use the tools in this book, 7 Pillars of Personal Change, mindfulness, mediation, breathing, zooming out, gratitude, self-acceptance, visualisation, journalling etc
- Recognise that you may fall off the wagon into codependent behaviour and use self-awareness to take yourself out of it again, remember baby steps
- Begin the journey to self-love by taking better care of yourself, working on perfectionist behaviour, your internal slave driver and internal critic and letting go of any guilt and shame
- Take an assertiveness course or practice being more assertive
- Take full responsibility for yourself, your feelings and your actions
- Communicate what you want and don't want clearly

- Set boundaries with the people around you as to what is acceptable or not, if someone regularly takes you for granted for example you could tell them that it is no longer acceptable for them to behave that way towards you
- Do a conflict resolution course or practice holding your ground in conflict situations, always making sure that you are in a safe environment to be able to do this
- Recognise and understand the person or persons you were codependent to and their own addictions including any of their codependent behaviour
- Begin the process of feeling comfortable with intimacy
- Continue the journey to your true self and self-love

Narcissism

Many of you may have heard about narcissism and it does seem to be a term that is banded around a lot, I will try to demystify the concept. In a very basic way many people think of narcissism as someone who thinks a lot of themselves, is often obsessed about their appearance and only sees how events and situations affect them. This simple definition is true however it is far more complex than that and there are levels of narcissism that someone may have. The Oxford dictionary defines narcissism as 'Selfishness, involving a sense of entitlement, a lack of empathy, and a need for admiration, as characterising a personality type.'

Earlier in the book I talked about the ego and its role in our lives, the ego is there to keep us from harm and is an integral part of our physical life. I will go as far as to say that all egos are low level narcissistic in nature, they focus purely on the self, are self-reflective, selfish and need to be seen and heard. Materialism is also important for level

1 narcissists and this is where we see 'keeping up with the Joneses', fakeness and superficial behaviour.

If the ego is balanced with the heart and intuition and connected to the true self then the traits of narcissism do not come forward however if there is a disconnection between the true self and the ego then these traits do come forward and can develop to the next level. Examples of this can be seen in how a lot of the population behave, a lot are primarily focused on themselves, how everything affects them and those they love and there is often a lack of empathy, understanding and support for other peoples' plight. This changes when there is a tragedy or disaster, when something like this happens it is the heart that sees and feels what has happened and is empathetic. This is why we often see the best in people during times of crisis.

The lack of balance between ego and heart is caused by a person only seeing themselves as the body that they are in, the belief that life has little meaning, the belief that thoughts define you and emotions are all there is to the human experience. This leads to a feeling of emptiness inside, a lack of self-worth, lack of self-love, judgemental behaviour and a need to put on an external front or persona to show the outside world something different to what is felt within. The ego is fully in charge in these situations and will easily go into fear and fight or flight mode.

If there is trauma in childhood and the inner child is deeply wounded and if there is a lack of connection between the true self and the ego then this can cause level 1 narcissistic traits to increase to higher levels. There are of course other personality disorders and traumas that can also lead to higher levels of narcissistic behaviour but issues in childhood are often the root cause.

Higher levels of narcissistic behaviour can be very challenging to deal with and when you are with someone who has that behaviour in a close relationship such as a partner, family member or coworker it can be very traumatic. Narcissistic abuse can seriously affect your mental health and deeply affects your self-esteem and emotional wellbeing. Narcissistic abuse is subtle and a victim of a narcissist can often feel like it is their fault that things happen due to their perceived shortcomings but this is just a symptom of the abuse. One of the ways that a narcissist will attract you is with their outward persona. They are often charismatic, they will say all the things that you think you want to hear, they will at first make you feel very special and you will think that you have met your soulmate, this however is not the case.

It is important to actually recognise that you are in a relationship with a narcissist and recognising the signs will help to do that, here are some to look out for:

- They live in their own world and do not relate to other people and society in the way other people do, they live in a fantasy world
- They lie and believe their own lies
- They need to control everything
- They are often perfectionistic
- They come across as superior and better than everyone else
- They think they are entitled to everything handed to them on a plate
- They need constant attention and have to be at the centre of every conversation and activity
- They take no responsibility for themselves or their actions, everything is always everyone else's fault
- They will almost never apologise for their behaviour unless they are trying to win you back to their

narcissistic view, an apology will always be a part of the game plan
- They often have childlike behaviour and will 'throw their toys out of their pram' if they do not get what they want
- They have no empathy towards other people, they don't feel guilt
- They think that everyone should think, believe and see things how they do, there is no room for another opinion
- They won't take no for an answer. They will try a range of strategies until they have finally worn you down to say yes
- They will not express how they feel, they expect you to be a mind reader. If you challenge them in any way they will become very defensive, they cannot communicate how they truly feel at all. They are poor at reading body language and interpreting other people's behaviour. Sarcasm is often lost on them
- You cannot reason with them nor can you use logical deduction or appeal to emotional understanding, they have none. You will never win an argument
- They exist in fear, every action that they take is done so because of fear, they exist in an almost constant state of anxiety
- They have deep repressed shame that affects their behaviour, causes them to be deeply judgemental of others
- They will never be their true self with you because they will never want you to see their faults
- They will not fully trust you thinking that one day you will let them down

There are of course many more examples but I am sure you can get an idea from these. It is also important to know what a narcissist will do in a relationship, here are some of the things you will observe:

- They will hone in on any insecurities you have, lack of self-esteem and any trauma you have experienced with the core purpose of making you even more insecure
- They will isolate you from everyone you love and make sure you have no friends
- They will do everything they can to make sure that you depend on them fully as long as they deign to provide
- Everything will be all your fault, always
- Sex will be one-sided, you will give it to them when they want and it will all be about their pleasure
- They will have you convinced that you are the one at fault and you are the one that needs to change
- They will make you question your whole reality
- They will be nice to you just enough to make you want to stay with them
- They will use your weaknesses against you
- If you try to hold them accountable for their behaviour they will act aggressively or extremely towards you
- They may well be jealous of you particularly if they are your parent
- They will fall out with people, cause a drama and upset
- They will belittle you in front of other people
- They will be secretive and keep sections of their life from you

The level of narcissism can increase and the abuse that they dish out can get worse. My advice would always be to get support from a professional and work towards leaving the relationship. If they are a family member it can be more difficult but you need to do what is right for you and if that means distancing yourself from them that is what you must do. Working on the activities in this book will help you to support your recovery from a narcissistic relationship.

The purpose of discussing self-sabotage, codependency and narcissism is to raise your awareness (Pillar 1) and allow you the opportunity to highlight changes that you need to make in your life. If at any point the amount that you need to change becomes overwhelming, which is common, you need to take some time to sit quietly and listen to your heart's guidance, your intuition in order to identify the things you can start with to change. The things that will have an impact on a number of areas of your life and the things that feel comfortable according to the stage that you are at. Journalling can also be a good way to work things out.

Feminine & Masculine Balance

As I discussed in the last section every one of us is a mix of masculine and feminine energy and the best way in which we function whether male or female or non binary is to have an EQUAL BALANCE of both masculine and feminine energy. Tao teacher Mantak Chia explains this need for balance well 'when male and female chi energies are balanced in the body, each cell will have the energy to function perfectly.' This has nothing to do with sexuality but to do with behaviour and energy and getting the best from life and being healthy mentally, physically, and emotionally as well as spiritually. Indeed the key to happy relationships whether they are intimate, family or friends is to create this balance within you. You will now see two sets of lists one for wounded masculine and feminine traits and one for divine feminine and masculine traits. Use these lists to help you to identify where you are currently and to write down areas that you want to work on, you may also like to journal about it.

The following traits or behaviours you may recognise in yourself or other people:

Wounded Feminine (Present in both genders)

- Often insecure
- Looks for confirmation from others about themselves and needy (appearance is an example)
- Can seem fake, insincere
- Is overly critical of others
- Can act and enjoy the role of victim deliberately putting others before themselves to their detriment
- Can become over emotional and is quick to share their feelings with others
- They are searching for love constantly can be clingy and suffocating in relationships
- Can be overtly critical and manipulative in order to get the love they think they need
- They are often co-dependent and self-sabotage
- Creative ideas do not manifest into reality
- Fails to get things done, procrastinates, has a tendency towards laziness
- Actions are taken based on fear-based consciousness

- Lack of sex drive
- Sexual contact and intimacy lacks connection to the heart energy and unconditional love

Wounded Masculine (Present in both genders)

- Often critical and judgemental of others
- Has to always be right and can be very defensive and goes into attack mode
- Cannot take criticism and fears failure and fails to listen
- Can have narcissistic tendencies which breed selfishness and arrogance
- Is very competitive and has to win, is only goal and success focussed
- Has a tendency towards addiction
- Mind focussed, extremely analytical and is not connected to their emotions
- Can be scared of love and can create deliberate separation as a result of fear
- Anger is prevalent, impatience with self and others
- Actions are taken based on fear-based consciousness
- Sexual contact and intimacy lacks connection to the heart energy and unconditional love
- Sex drive for gratification only

Divine Feminine (Present in both genders)

- Openly loving, trusting and empathetic
- Surrenders to vulnerability
- Naturally uses intuition listening to the heart before the mind
- Projects beauty with a glowing flow of light energy
- Speaks their mind in an authentic way without shame
- Creates boundaries, is strong but gracious
- Is comfortable in their physical body

- Is naturally creative, ideas flow effortlessly
- Is capable of deep intimacy and unconditional love
- Sexual contact is equal, expressive, sensual and deeply loving

Divine Masculine (Present in both genders)

- Is mindful, grounded and present and is fully aware of self and others
- Is non-judgemental
- Has high integrity
- Makes decisions for the highest good of all involved
- Takes responsibility and is accountable for their actions
- Is disciplined and focussed when required
- Is authentically humble but confident and open to learning
- Is able to take ideas and manifest them into reality
- Is capable of deep intimacy and unconditional love
- Sexual contact is equal, expressive, sensual and deeply loving

You may have been able to identify some traits in yourself within all 4 areas, or just some from two or three, the goal for anyone is to be able to create a balance between their masculine and feminine energies. **You would expect to have the traits of both the divine feminine and divine masculine whatever your gender.**

People who have wounded traits tend to be drawn to other people who have the traits that they are lacking OR traits that suit their own wounding. For example a man who has wounded masculine traits and a lack of divine feminine traits may be attracted to a woman who has wounded feminine traits, the controlling fear-based competitive man is attractive to the needy, victim, codependent woman who feels the man can keep her safe, she can 'save him' and put him above her own needs. These traits are initially attractive to the man who feels she will be easily controlled and will do exactly what he wants. However this is a recipe for disaster as her clingy, over emotional ways stifle him and he turns to anger, resentment and this can lead to violence.

The vital message here is that I do not want you to get hung up on your gender, the important part is to have (or be working towards) a balance of BOTH divine masculine and divine feminine energy traits. Think of it as an internal marriage, the coming together of your masculine and feminine sides in an equal union that will create harmony from within and project outwards.

As we all are aware there are different degrees of masculinity and femininity within the genders, some men are very masculine physically and in the way that they carry themselves and the same with women who are deeply feminine however there are then varying degrees of that within both genders. It is common that a strongly masculine man will search out a deeply feminine woman to help him to create balance and visa versa. Equally a more feminine man may be attracted to a more masculine woman (or masculine man if they are homosexual) and so on. The thing to remember here is creating balance within will support and help you whatever and whoever you are and that will support the building of successful relationships with whomever you choose to be with. The union of masculine and feminine energies are always wanting to create balance.

After that, you are in the right position to make decisions about what you choose for your life, this could be to grow with a current partner, decide that your current relationship is not right, you may decide to be on your own, or in a heterosexual or homosexual relationship or any other variation of relationship that is right for you. Being balanced in both masculine and feminine energies gives you the opportunity to choose. Individuals who are balanced in their energies attract people who are like themselves and so there is a greater chance of successful relationships happening. Everyone is unique and loving your own individual expression of humanity is the path to self-mastery.

Body Image

The mainstream media including magazines, movies, TV shows including reality TV programmes and on social media commonly show both the female and male bodies as 'perfect', thin men and women with six packs etc . This can lead many people, particularly young people to think and feel that they have to look like the people they see in the media. Many photographs and videos are airbrushed or edited in order to make the model or actor look better than they actually do. Actors and models who are depicted this way, it is their job and their career and the amount of time they spend exercising and in the gym and eating a particular way relates to an investment in their career because they have to look a certain way to get jobs. This is not however the reality for the average person and it is important to recognise this. Whatever your body looks like you have to be happy with it but it does not mean it has to be perfect. Do not allow media depictions of other people's bodies make you feel shame about your own body. It is okay to want a six pack and to put the work in to achieve that as long as it is for your own self-love and not so you can impress others or try to live up to false societal expectations. Having a healthy body is the most important thing.

Moving our bodies for balance

We all know from government guidelines that certain amount of exercise is good for our health and can support overall well-being and as discussed earlier the connection between your mind and your body is also vital to good health and to your self-development. This does not mean hours spent on a treadmill or pumping weights in a gym. It does mean spending dedicated time on a daily basis connecting with your breath and your body and moving your body to keep it supple and fit for purpose. Much like a car, the body's perfect design needs regular use and maintenance for it to keep working.

This may seem daunting to you particularly if you do not really do any form of exercise at all. The core of what you need to do is to connect your mind to your body through being present when doing the exercise. Using breath to not only focus on being present but to ensure that you get enough oxygen to your muscles and to promote the flow of energy through the bloodstream and to excrete carbon dioxide. Many people are so focussed on the exercise they are doing that they forget about correct breathing and this can cause issues. Of course panting and double breathing during strenuous exercise is normal but if you can focus on your breath during this time it will help you to recover more quickly and increase your ability to do the exercise; this is about being mindful, being present, mindful exercise and mindful breathing during the exercise.

Another important part of exercising is using the mind to focus on the muscles that are being used during the exercise. Let's say that you are doing a set of sit-ups. If you focus your mind on the abdominal muscles that you are using this can increase the effectiveness of the sets done.

Dedicating time for warm up to allow yourself the opportunity to breath properly, settle into your exercise space and become mindful and present can help in the process of connecting the mind to the body for exercise. If you are not experienced at a particular type of exercise then doing it more slowly helps you to focus the mind and body connection. Yoga is a good example of this, in the western world often the mind, body, and spirit benefits are not realised and the poses are just seen as stretching exercises. However getting in the pose or asana and mindfully focusing on the pose, the muscles being used, and using the correct breathing increases the mind and body connection and then the effectiveness of the pose on the physical body.

There is a theme to much of what I am talking about in this book and that is about balance. Learning how to get the right amount of body movement for you can be achieved through listening to your body, that goes for other aspects too including eating and health and I will pick up on those later. The more that you develop the mind and body connection the more that you will be in tune with what your body wants and needs.

When thinking about your body movement and exercise regime you need a starting point, where are you at now? What are your medical and physical limitations? Do you need to consult your medical practitioner before deciding on any type of exercise ? (recommended). Here are some suggestions, feel free to research and find what suits you best :

- Dog walking, this may be something that you do already however, try it in a different way. Do not look at your mobile phone whilst you are out. Practice being present, connect to your breathing. Notice how your body feels during the walk, take a much closer notice of your surroundings. If you're able to walk in nature this can also be extremely beneficial. (the walk need not be with a dog if you do not own one.)

- Yoga is a wonderful way to stretch and exercise your body, if you are senior or have some form of disability there are a lot of free videos on YouTube just for you, chair or wheelchair yoga are available as are slow and gentle versions.
- Yoga classes, I personally use Les Mills Body Balance classes (lesmills.com) which is a great mix of Tai Chi, Yoga and Pilates and can be done at accredited classes or streamed On Demand. There are also lots of people now offering yoga classes. Whoever you choose to go with please remember to follow the key points I made earlier about being present, using your breath and connecting the mind and the body.
- You may be a regular runner on the streets, hiker, treadmill user, weight lifter, or cyclist. Whatever it is that you do, please review how present you are during the exercise, how effectively you use your breath and how strong your mind and body connection is and make adjustments accordingly.
- Maybe you are exercising a lot, out running daily or in the gym mosts days, if this is the case then evaluate your motivation for doing this. Is it so you can have a great body so you can feel good enough for partners or attractive to a potential partner if you are single? Is it just for good health or are there other reasons? Is this level of exercise giving you time to do other things that will bring you balance? I am not saying that exercising 6 or 7 times a week is not good but I encourage you to review.
- You may also want to look at the types of exercise you do, varying physical movement is important, running one day, doing yoga another and lifting weights another may give you a good balance.

Review your own practices and use the 7 Pillars of Change to shift your behaviour to a more mind, body, and spirit based approach. Looking after your physical body is vitally important in your journey of self-discovery and personal growth. Remember to consult a professional before starting something new and use your increased mind and body connection to listen to what your body needs, days vary and flexibility is very important. Some days we don't feel like exercising and then push ourselves to do it and feel much better from it but other days our bodies are screaming NO! Being able to tell the difference is really important.

Mindful Eating, Food, and Nutrition

The more that you become present and connect your mind to your body, the more you can 'listen' to what your body is telling you. This will take a number of different forms including identifying areas for physical healing, and the ability to truly listen to what your body is telling you it wants to eat, drink, how much and when. When your body needs to exercise, when it needs to rest, when it needs to meditate and so on. You may also find that as you move along the path of your awakening journey that your tastes will change and what you body needs at different stages will change also.

Most of us have patterns of behaviour in our relationship with food that include some or all of the following:

- As discussed previously, we believe that we deserve to have an item of food such as a sweet treat (chocolate, ice cream, biscuits etc.) or a glass of wine
- We believe that we don't have enough money to afford to eat healthily
- We believe we don't have time to cook healthily

- We believe that we can't cook well and do not know how to cook more healthily
- Our bodies are caught in a cycle of glucose yoyo, where the sugar levels go high and then plummet low
- We believe that we have to finish all the food on our plate because of how much the food cost
- We believe that we have to finish all the food on our plate because it is a waste to throw it away
- We are not prepared to try new foods because we instantly believe that we do not or will not like them
- We believe we do not like certain foods because our parents or partner does not
- We believe if we eat too much we will get fat

False Messages

We can often get false messages from our body about what we want to consume, often hunger is mixed up with thirst. We will crave sweet things when our sugar levels are low but consuming those items will then make the glucose yoyo worse. Our emotional state will also affect the messages we receive from our bodies. Stress will send us into behaviour patterns that lead us to addictive foods, upset, arguments, tiredness etc will also do the same. If you give the body healthier food when it is used to more processed or animal based food it will cause a reaction giving off a false message that the healthy food does not suit. The toxins in your body that have been ingested through the eating of processed foods and foods sprayed with pesticides (and the like) do not like it when you do not eat those foods because effectively you are starving them and so they will send false messages to eat those foods.

Another thing that can cause poor eating habits is boredom. If you are not happy in your life, are restricted by circumstances, or not happy in a job for example, you can easily get bored and that can lead to eating for the sake of eating. Nibbling on snacks of unhealthy food that brings comfort gives you something to do.

Mindful eating is being so connected to your body that you can listen to what it tells you, and then make good choices about what you eat, drink and put into your body. You need to recognise what emotional state you are in as a part of the process of being mindful.

Some guidelines about food:

- As discussed everything is energy and that includes food and drink
- Anything plant-based has a high energy vibration
- Animal and seafood flesh have a lower energy vibration
- Processed food has a lower energy vibration
- Sugar drinks have a low energy vibration
- Processed sugar in general affects the body's ability to regulate sugar and excessive consumption commonly leads to diabetes or pre-diabetic symptoms
- Plant-based food integrates with the body in a seamless way
- Each individual body is unique and requires different nutrition at different times of day
- Your body does like water so if you're not a fan of water try to get creative about how to drink water, sparkling with slices of fruit in it is a great way to have a tasty drink with no additives or caffeine
- When changing diets there is a detox process that occurs. This process creates side effects, but they will pass as the body adjusts to what it wants and needs to consume

- Also note that having a little something sweet or a glass of wine is fine. What you are looking for are patterns that lead to this type of eating or drinking. Have a chocolate bar because you would like it, not because you think you deserve it. Have a glass of wine to enjoy the taste, to not to relax or relieve stress.

I'm not advocating any particular type or style of diet here, and I do not want to make anyone feel bad for what they consume in their diet. I raise these points as part of Pillar 1 of the 7 pillars of change, to raise your self-awareness in your relationship with food. What behaviours can you identify with yourself ? Research good places, reliable sources to learn more about food, where it comes from, and how it is produced. Ultimately the key here is to listen to your body, doing the following exercise may help you in this process:

Take 3 deep breaths and transfer your awareness from your mind to your body. Ask your body what food it needs to eat, do not try to force any images to come to you, just allow them to flow and see what arises. What you will find is the first images that come are what you body wants and needs, you may be surprised that it is drink instead of food for example. This is something to practice as you will get better at it. If you see food that seems to be unsuitable it could be because you need to practice more or that your body needs that food at that moment, just beware of false messages.

When you have eaten something, review whether or not it settled well in your system and did it go through easily without discomfort, or did it upset your system in some way? If you eat several things, try to ask your body what it was that upset you so that you know to avoid it next time. Often it is a process of trial and error, sometimes you may do this naturally but going deeper into it will help you to find the right balance of food and drink for you. You should also notice what your body is asking for at different times of day, week, month, and after exercise. Remember your body is unique and you need to find what is right for you.

I found doing this exercise helped me to have more energy and to be more productive, to cleanse and clear out negativity. I have been vegetarian for over 25 years but still did not have a great diet. Using this process together with being well informed about what I was eating helped to improve my diet and well being considerably. The more I went down my spiritual path I noticed that lower energy food tended to keep me bogged down in a lower vibration and all that comes with it, when I eat higher vibration food (plant based) I have a higher vibration and feel far more connected to everything around me, feeling much more balanced and alive.

There is a lot of misinformation out there about diets (and exercise programmes), if you are looking for help and guidance, research thoroughly, ask yourself who is behind the research, many research studies are funded by pharmaceutical companies and food manufacturers, with the sole purpose of getting the results they want to convince us that eating this food is good or not. Their agenda is to sell their product and make money. The information is often conflicting and indeed opposite advice is often given from one research study to another. Again finding your own truth is important and being mindful and listening to your intuition will go a long way in supporting your evaluation of what is right for you.

Cleansing

The reality of the world that we live in is that we are exposed to a wide range of toxins, pollutants and poisons. They are all around us, in our homes, in the food we eat, in the air we breathe, the water we drink and bathe in, the health and beauty products we use, and the medication used in traditional medicine. All of these toxins, pollutants and poisons build up in the cells of the body and particularly in the organs that filter, the liver and the kidneys or with hormone producing glands like the thyroid and the pineal gland. Indeed they can be passed on through DNA in the egg and sperm into the cells of children. Toxins build up in our systems from multiple lifetimes. They are in our genetic DNA but can be removed.

Many illnesses manifest in the body as a result of these toxins, pollutants and poisons and the body trying to cope with them. Many people get 24-48 hour so-called bugs that are just the body detoxifying itself.

I personally have experienced periods of time when I started feeling not poorly but not well, stomach upset a little, headache, tiredness and that was followed by a severe attack of migraine and sickness when my body purged stored toxins and released them. Afterwards I would always feel much better and I began to realise that rather than get to the stage where I was physically unwell I needed to cleanse the body myself.

There are a lot of different types of cleanses and lots of information and misinformation about the benefits and drawbacks of cleansing, again when researching, look at who is behind the information. I personally recommend Anthony William and his Medical Medium series. He has a lot of fantastic information and a range of different cleanses and recipes to help with the cleansing process. By doing a regular cleanse you can help purge your body of built up toxins but it is also wise to look at what you consume and use on your body on a daily basis to reduce the amount of toxins going into and throughout your system.

How and When to Eat

There are other factors to consider that are linked to mindful eating. In our busy lives many of us do not eat properly and often multitask when eating and this can cause a number of the following issues :

- Eating too much because the message that the stomach is full is missed
- Not chewing food properly
- The overeating and not chewing then causes heartburn, ingestion and flatulence
- Not tasting the food that is being eaten
- Not noticing if food is not fresh and eating something that has started to go off
- Not eating until the evening
- Not eating at regular enough intervals, our bodies copes much better with little and often and is less likely to store for future energy needs

If you want to enjoy food and actually taste the beautiful food you eat:

- Dedicate time to eat properly
- Chew your food fully with small mouthfuls
- When your stomach tells you that its full stop eating (it commonly takes 20 minutes for the message to get from the stomach to the brain that it is full
- Eat regularly, small and often

Not eating for at least 4 hours before going to bed so that the digestive system has a break and leaves the body free to heal itself during the period that you are asleep is also a great idea. This fast is also conducive to a more restful sleep.

Forgiveness

Forgiveness is a powerful way of helping you to recover from any type of trauma. It is common for us to blame ourselves for things that have happened; we didn't do enough, we did something that caused it, we think we deserve it and so on. Bringing forth the realisation that whatever happened and whoever was to blame does not serve you in the present and forgiving yourself for anything that you feel you might have done that led to or during any traumatic event will bring you a greater feeling of peace about what happened to you. The following self-forgiveness practice can help you on your journey of self-forgiveness, remember that forgiveness is an energy and bringing that energy forward will help to heal you.

Self-forgiveness Practice

Find a comfortable position in a place where you will not be disturbed and take 3 deep breaths, close your eyes and take your awareness from your mind to your heart space. Focus on your breathing in and out through the nose. Then in your mind's eye visualise a beautiful waterfall that cascades down into an aquamarine pool of water. Go and step into the pool of water, you will feel that it is cool but refreshing. You will feel the water seep through your skin and into your body, bringing forth cleansing energy. Place your hand over your heart centre and say I forgive myself, I forgive myself, I forgive myself.

You then walk and stand underneath the waterfall. The water flows over you bringing healing and compassion, forgiveness and peace. You stand for a while letting this wonderful feeling wash over you. Now walk out of the pool and back onto dry ground, all of your clothes, skin and hair are dry, you feel much lighter now, the washing away of the pain through the practice of forgiveness has created more room in your heart to bring forth more love for yourself.

You can do this short visualisation practice as many times as you need to in order to let go and forgive yourself. You may want to focus on just one thing or event each time you do the practice.

Removing Self-judgement

As discussed previously, many people often feel that their thoughts define them, that their thoughts make them the people they are, if they have bad thoughts then they think they must be bad people. If the bad thoughts are about themselves then they also tend to believe them and that leads to a vicious circle of thought sickness. As the mind and body are connected, thought sickness then becomes physical sickness and as the body feels pain it makes the overall person feel worse.

Self-Judgemental thoughts are like a virus, they infect the mind and then create behaviours and situations in life that mirror the thoughts produced. These self-judgemental thoughts then take on a life of their own and are then used by the ego to 'protect' from harm, and the resulting behaviour becomes the new normal. When this goes on for some time the behaviour and thoughts are then pushed into the subconscious mind and become a way of life. The image of the self then becomes distorted and then this image is believed to be a part of the personality.

Using the 7 Pillars of Personal Change is really important to identify a link between self-judgemental thoughts and patterns of behaviour, Pillar 4 challenging beliefs is particularly important here, using the Challenging Beliefs Exercise (on page 63) will also help. The most important thing is if you identify self-judgemental thoughts that you do not go back into the pattern of judging yourself for having them. You need to step away from what is happening, a bit like the lens of a camera, zooming in and out of the situation to identify the truth of what is going on for you without judging yourself.

Zooming Out Exercise (linked to Pillar 3 Making Sense)

After using Pillars 1 and 2 identify a pattern of behaviour that is linked to self-judgemental thoughts, think about a situation where you acted using this behaviour. Once you have a specific example, sit down, take three deep breaths and close your eyes and visualise the situation in your mind's eye. Notice as many aspects that you can from your personal perspective, your thoughts, emotions, feelings (where in the body you felt them), someone else's reaction to you and your reaction back, the place it happened, the triggers for it and so on. Once you have done that if you feel the need to, write it down.

Next, take another three deep breaths and imagine yourself sitting in a theatre, you are at the front centre and the play is the situation you just went through. This time when the actors play out the scene you will look at it as a separate person viewing the situation from the outside. This time you observe what you see, the emotions, the body language, how other people react to you and your reaction in return. If you feel you need to write it down, then do so. Then go onto observe the differences between the two, one when you are in the situation and one when you are observing it from outside. It should give you a number of insights into the reality of how you are behaving rather than your perception of it and will give you a good idea of what the self-judgemental thoughts are and the behaviour that they are causing.

Gratitude Practice

You may have heard about gratitude practices and you should not underestimate the power of such practices. Gratitude and appreciation are very positive energy practices that can deeply shift your daily psyche from negative thought patterns to positive ones.

Choose a time of day that suits you, I tend to do this in the evening before bed but it may set up your day by doing it in the mornings so choose what works best for you. Say out loud the things that you are grateful for in your life, this includes some of the simple things that we often take for granted these things could include:

- Grateful for your partner, home, food
- Grateful for an interaction with someone
- Grateful for a book you are reading, a programme you are watching, movie you saw
- Grateful for the way you handled a difficult situation

The gratitude practice could include anything that you are happy about; purely by focusing on the positive things in your life brings forth an immense amount of positive energy that dispels negative thoughts and bring a much deeper sense of calm into the body and mind. As with any routine, you need to establish it and to remember to do this daily you will need to plan it into your routine for the day like you would brushing your teeth. This practice has had a huge impact for me personally particularly when I was having some very difficult days focusing on what was good in my life and bringing forth that positivity made it a lot easier to cope and manage the challenging times.

Grounding Exercise

What is grounding? Grounding is feeling fully in your body, connected to the earth and your surroundings. When meditating or visioning it is important to remain grounded during the process. Symptoms of not being grounded include:

- Lightheadedness
- Fuzzy or foggy-headed
- Blurry vision
- Poor concentration
- Tiredness
- Nausea

If you feel that you are not grounded or are going to meditate or visualise then you can use the following grounding exercise:

Close your eyes and take three long deep breaths, scan down your body and focus in on your energy centres. Go to the energy centre at the base of your spine (root chakra) and visualise a cord going from your root chakra through the floor, down into the ground, and deep into the core of Mother Earth. This cord helps to ground you and also allows for you to receive energy from Mother Earth herself. You may also like to use a grounding crystal such as black tourmaline.

Breathing

Breathing may sound simple, breath is 'the breath of life'; it is also a way to bring in peace and let go of negativity. Breath is also healing and aids the body's natural healing process. Breath also helps with concentration and focus.

Spending so much time on autopilot we commonly only shallow breathe and do not get enough oxygen into our bodies for healing, health and vitality. Correct breathing technique is also really important when doing any form of exercise and can improve the quality and results gained from any workout.

Focussing on your breath actively reduces stress levels, lowers the heart rate and brings calm to the body.

Focussed breathing is also a very good place to start when starting your journey in coming off autopilot and being more present.

Exercises to do:

Focus on your breathing, notice how you are breathing, often we breathe in a shallow way and the more anxious or stressed we are the less we breathe correctly. Observe first how you are breathing and at different times. Is it worse when you are worried or stressed?

Breathing to come off autopilot and create calm:

Find a comfortable place to sit where you will not be disturbed. This could be at home, in the workplace or outside on a bench. I find closing my eyes works for me but you do not have to, do whatever works for you. Notice how your breathing is at first, then begin to focus on your breath. Take 3 large diaphragmatic breaths in and out, when breathing out let as much air out as you can. There are lots of theories about breathing, count so many in, count so many on hold, count so many going out. My personal experience trying different methods was, firstly too much breath in and I started to get tingles in my fingers, holding for too long did not feel good, and concentrating too much on the counting stopped me from relaxing. Although practice to help me to improve.

The key here is to do what works for you, the goal is to create calm and peace for a few minutes. If deep breathing, holding and counting works do it! If it doesn't, don't worry, what you need to do is focus on your breathing, ensuring you are getting full lungs of air and creating calm. Try initially for just a few minutes, if you can do 5 minutes a day, three times a day, that would be a great start.

Once you have mastered focussed breathing for a few minutes a few times a day you will start to notice that it brings you a sense of calm. Consistency is important and I know that can be a challenge for many people, getting caught up in doing and remembering to take your 5 minutes breathing time, if you forget please do not start feeling negative about yourself or what you are trying to achieve. Changing behaviour is a challenge and everyone needs to start somewhere. The minute you beat yourself up about forgetting or not doing your practice, it creates negativity around the behaviour and will lead to you possibility of giving up.

Breathe and affirmation to let go of negativity and blocked emotions :

This exercise can be done either sitting or lying down, make sure that you will not be disturbed whilst you are doing it. Focus on your breath, take 3 large diaphragmatic breaths in and out, when breathing out let as much air out as you can. Close your eyes and keep focusing on your breath, during this time you may find thoughts come into your mind, this is normal, your mind is designed to think, just allow the thoughts to come and then let them go, do not get caught up in the thoughts, this will stop your focus on the breath. If you drift, go back to your breath and start again, and do not judge yourself or think you are doing anything wrong if you do this it just creates negativity. Focus on your breathing again and keep this going for a few minutes, allow your body to relax, if focussing on each part of your body and helps you do this then do it.

Once you are relaxed take your focus from your head to your heart space and then do the following :

Breathing in say out loud or silently "I breathe in positivity"

Breathing out say " I breathe out negativity"

Breathing in say " I breathe in love"

Breathing out say " I breathe out anger"

Breathing in say " I breathe in peace"

Breathing out say " I breathe out all emotions that are blocked and do not serve me"

Repeat these three times and then go back to focusing on your breathing for a few more minutes. If you know what it is that you want to release then insert that into the example above accordingly.

What this exercise does is gets you used to using the energy of these words, the energy of positivity, the energy of love etc. to change your state and feel better, calmer and healthier.

Belly Breathing

Belly breathing is another really good way to help you to relax and bring you calm and to be mindful. It is very simple to do: Lie on your back and place one hand on your chest and one hand on your belly, focus on your breathing and the goal is to not let the chest move at all and for all your breathing to be done from the stomach area. Once you have achieved only belly breathing then go onto focus on breathing in to the count of 8 then let go of the breath slowly to the count of 5. Keep doing this and notice how the rest of your body begins to really relax.

Body Scan

Body scan is a type of meditation where you focus on the different parts of your body to identify any blocks in energy or physical issues that may need addressing. This is really useful to do about once a week to check to see how your body is, once you start to get physical symptoms of something it can often mean that the issue has been developing for a while, by doing a body scan you can help you to identify issues and start to work on them in the early stages. Performing a body scan can also help you to develop a better relationship with your body; most of us are not happy with at least certain parts of our physical body and we can be very negative towards it, doing the body scan helps to become more positive and starts to build a healthier relationship with our physical self. Performing a body scan:

- Lie down on a yoga mat or bed and get comfortable, make sure you have warm enough clothes on, and make sure that your neck is comfortable
- Close your eyes and focus on your breathing using the belly breathing method
- Become aware of how the floor or bed feels against your body
- Move your focus from your belly to your left foot, start by observing the toes, including the bones,

ligaments, and skin, notice how they feel and what sensations you feel, are there issues?

- Then move up the left side of your body doing the same thing with the rest of your leg, arm and keep moving around the body from left to right
- Having a basic knowledge of your internal physiology is a good idea so you can check your liver, kidneys, heart and other organs
- You may simply identify tightness or tension in a muscle and can take action immediately by consciously working on relaxing that muscle

Inner Child

I knew that I needed to write about the inner child and our relationship with our them but as I continue my own journey back to my sovereign self I did not really connect with or understand my own inner child. It was whilst writing this book I asked my guides and spirit mentors to help me with my inner child so that I could authentically write about it and share my experience with you all. I had never felt like a child even when I was one, I always felt like an adult and struggled with letting go and really having fun, even on the occasions I did let go I could hear my adult self saying I should not be doing it. I did not want to have children and felt a lack of connection to them, I just did not understand them at all. As part of this journey of self-mastery and embodied sovereignty I knew that this was something I needed help with. During a meditation, with help from my spirit mentors I found my inner child, in the vision he was tied to a chair and had burn marks all over him, I saw lots of situations where he had been abused, scared, not loved, abandoned and hurt during my childhoods from many lifetimes. During the meditation I freed him from his shackles and healed his physical wounds. Afterwards the wave of emotions that hit me were huge and I cried deeply for his pain, my pain from my childhood. I now feel my inner child as an important aspect of my consciousness. It has not all been plain sailing though as sometimes I have been expressing bad childlike behaviour that has not been part of my personality before however I recognise that this is all part of the journey to heal my inner child. Positively I feel whole, the part of me that I did not know was missing has returned, I feel like I can have fun much more and feel a deeper connection to children.

Jacobson (2017) explains what the inner child is her explanation mirrors my own experience well 'The inner child reflects the child we once were in both his or her 'negative' and 'positive' aspects. Both our unmet needs and suppressed childhood emotions, as well as our childlike innocence, creativity and joy.'

Why is the relationship with and healing of your own inner child important?

Recognising that you have an inner child is the first step to understanding, healing and developing a relationship with your inner child. The child is a part of your subconscious, the wounded child that has stored up hurt, pain, wounds and needs not met from childhood. I am not suggesting here that all parents do a bad job but think of it like this.

As a parent you only tend to use your own experiences, knowledge and wisdom, you are also going through your own set of life lessons and challenges. A child does not have the adult view of the world, their view is innocent, simplistic and often black and white. So if mommy comes home in a bad mood the child does not know it's because of her boss who annoyed her, the child thinks that mommy is angry with it. This hurt or wound is stored into the subconscious mind and becomes part of the child personality of that person. This is just one example, if there is actual abuse be it, mental, emotional or physical (or all 3) then these wounds build on the hurt and wounds of the inner child.

I am sure all of you can relate to a situation similar to this:

You come home from work and your partner who finished work 2 hours before you has not started to make anything to eat, they are sitting watching TV, immediately you start shouting and asking them why they have not made dinner, your reaction is fairly extreme and you feel quite upset and full of emotion. Your partner is looking at you realising they had better not say anything or you will react further or they shout back and you end up having a heated argument.

What is really going here? Your reaction is that of your wounded inner child, at some point in your childhood something happened that caused you to feel hurt by a situation. The root cause emotion could be that you felt that you were not considered, or you were taken for granted, or that your needs were ignored. These may have been reenforced over a period of time and settled into the emotional storehouse of your inner child. As an adult when a similar situation arises to what happened to you as a child it is the inner child that speaks out.

Understanding why you react in the way that you do in such situations is a vital part of beginning to understand and having a relationship with your inner child.

Here are some ways in which you can start to develop and heal your relationship with your inner child:

- Firstly accept and recognise that you have an inner child
- Use the first three Pillars of Personal Change (raising awareness, observation, and making sense) to

recognise when your inner child is reacting and what the triggers for those reactions are

- Don't feel shame about your reactions because this will make you feel bad about yourself and is counter productive
- Meditate and ask your inner child what is happening and what the reasons for the reactions are - try to get to the route cause emotions
- Parent your inner child by recognising and accepting the feelings and emotions as they come up, your inner child likes to be seen, heard and recognised.
- Forgive your caregivers who caused the wounds to your inner child for the harm the they inflicted
- Use the guided meditation in the next section of the book
- Use The Pillars of Personal change 5,6 and 7 (deciding to change, testing new ways and adopting new ways) to heal inner child wounds and make changes to the way you react in adult situations
- Explain to your partner, family, and friends about your inner child wounding and how you are making changes to your current behaviour
- When you become much more aware of the reasons for your 'child like' reactions you can stop yourself from reacting when met with a trigger

How to work with your inner child in a positive way

As adults we go through life with all its ups and downs and coping with the highs and lows, we often become a little jaded and cynical in our view of the world. We forget how to use our childhood innocence to see things in a different way or how to tap into our creativity and sense fun and adventure. As children we are born with balanced masculine and feminine energy, it is the feminine energy in us all where our creativity comes from and as children we are able to tap into that easily, as adults we are conditioned otherwise and our masculine and feminine energy goes out of balance. Doing the following can help you with all of these elements:

- Mediate and meet your inner child, recognise him or her and ask them what they need, try to discover what wounds are the most painful so that you can bring them forth into your conscious mind
- Are you naturally a creative person or do you struggle with creativity? Whether you do or not it is a great idea before starting a creative project to meditate and ask your inner child to help you with your creativity, focus on that innocent wonderment and let the creative juices flow
- All of us like to have fun but often we find it difficult to free our developed inhibitions and really enjoy ourselves or require alcohol or drugs to do that for us. Tapping into inner child innocence really helps to enable us to let go and have fun. Remember how good it feels to laugh, dance, act daft and just let go without fear of being judged? Allow your inner child to guide you to activities that they like to do so that you can enjoy yourself more. These are important elements in balancing your mind, body, and spirit.

Tools to Support your Awakening

As a part of your journey of self-discovery there are a number of alternative and metaphysical practices that you can use to help you. It is my experience that many people who start walking the path of self-discovery are naturally drawn to one or more of these practices. It is important to remember that as human beings we are fully efficient self-healers. Healing is only blocked by a lack of mind, body, and spirit balance, that can be remedied by addressing all four parts of your being, physical, mental, emotional and spiritual bodies. The tasks, exercises, meditations, and recommendations in this book are all here to guide you to achieving that balance. You need to use a range of approaches for healing, just using crystals, or only exercising or using meditation alone, will not in themselves create mind, body, and spirit balance. Using a range of methods that are right for you will help you work towards that balance. It is your intuition through self-awareness and using the 7 Pillars of Personal Change that will guide you to which methods to use and when to use them on your awakening and healing journey. I am going to go through a few practices with a small amount of guidance on each one, many I have used myself on my journey.

Meditation

There is a lot of talk about meditation and how good it is for you, and all of the benefits are true including a huge reduction in stress and therefore the impact of stress levels including reduced risks of heart disease and cancer. Mediation brings you peace, calm, and it enables you to make good decisions, it connects you to your heart and through that to your true self.

When people think about meditation they see it as sitting cross-legged thinking about nothing for a long time. In reality meditation is a very personal thing and you need to find your own way of meditating, one that works for you. Try a few different methods and combination of methods until you find what suits you.

I found that the best way to start was to find somewhere comfortable to sit and get as comfortable as possible and take some deep breaths, initially in through the nose and out through the mouth, do this until you feel relaxed, continue to breath normally and focus on the breath. What you will find is that thoughts will come to your mind, this is of course normal, the mind is made to think. What we normally do is get caught up in those thoughts and allow one thought to lead to another and we judge ourselves when analysing these thoughts. When you are meditating try to allow those thoughts to just come and go and do not get caught up in them and bring your focus back to your breath; this type of meditation is known as mindfulness meditation.

There are other ways that you can get into a meditative state including:

- Concentration meditation involves focussing on an object for a period of time without becoming distracted or getting caught up in thoughts. One can use a crystal or a lit candle for example to concentrate on. You may want to use the OM mantra to help with the concentration. This mantra resonates with the frequency of your true self and this can help to find inner calm and peace.

- Guided meditation (like the ones I have included in this book), is when someone else guides you through visualisation to find that place of calm within you and connect to your true self. Guided meditations can also be used to elicit a change within by focusing on a particular subject, my inner child meditation is an example of this.
- Mantra or music as an aid to meditation can also help as discussed on page 121 music and its frequency can have a huge impact on the human brain. Choosing music that has a positive frequency can aid relaxation and support you in getting into a meditative state some examples include:
- Nature
- Chanting
- Drumming
- Binaural beats
- Tibetan singing bowls
- Harps
- Tuning forks
- Crystal healing bowls
- Various frequency Hertz music (see page 122)
- Transcendental meditation is often the ultimate goal for meditators where thought is transcended and no longer present during the meditation. It is during this state of higher consciousness that brings an individual much closer to their true self and enables communication with higher realms.

What I have found is that sometimes using a number of different methods of mediation combined together can work really effectively at getting into a higher state of consciousness. Using all of the 5 physical senses can work well in achieving this. Here are a couple of examples of how I use these methods to meditate:

- I take a bath using water that is not too hot and place healing salts into the water, I light candles, burn incense, and listen to relaxing 438 hertz music. In this way I am using all 5 of my physical senses to create a suitable atmosphere to meditate. I do close my physical eyes in order to open my third eye to mediate so exchange my sight sense for my sixth sense. This method may not work for everyone because some people require no sound for example or may not like smells.
- Another way that helps me to meditate is when I am physically moving my body. I love to use a cross trainer machine to run and will put on music (headphones usually) and close my eyes and just run. I use my third eye to get into a deep meditation and often vision during these sessions. 30 minutes or more can go by and I do not recall the actual exercise at all and at the end I feel a very deep sense of calm and have exhilarating energy.
- I will also simply sit next to a tree or in the garden or by my sacred space inside and breathe and be.

The key message about meditation is that there is no right or wrong, it takes practice even if you only manage 5 minutes to begin with that is fine, consistency is the key. If you wander off into thought land then DO NOT beat yourself up and say that you have failed, simply go back to the breathing exercises and begin again. Try different methods, different times of day and see what works for you, BUT do meditate as often as possible, freeing up that time will save you more time in the long run. It needs to be something that you have to initially make the effort to do and then it will transition into being a part of your daily routine much like brushing your teeth is now. You'll be amazed how much meditating can transform your life, get past the need to be busy all the time, get off autopilot and just BE.

Affirmations

Affirmations are positive statements that we say to ourselves to shift the from negative thought patterns to positive thought patterns, negative energy to positive energy with your mind. I have written some examples of affirmations that you could use but it is easy to write them for yourself. Once you have identified some of your negative thought patterns are and false beliefs, using the 7 Pillars of Personal Change, you can write positive statements and say them to yourself on a daily or multiple daily basis. You can also say them during the breathing exercise (on pages 97 - 100). Only work on a few affirmations at a time and when you have used one or two for a while you will feel a shift within you that will indicate that affirmation has landed within you and then you can move onto the next one or two.

Health

I feel well today, my body is fully operational and works to the best of its capabilities.

I have the energy I need to complete the work and play that I want to do today.

I am in touch with the flow of my body's rhythm and I will respond to that rhythm with positive intent.

Abundance

I am abundant; I am open to all avenues of prosperity and understand that prosperity may come in many different forms.

I have an unlimited abundance of love.

I have an unlimited abundance of health.

I have an unlimited abundance of energy.

I have an unlimited abundance of positive thought.

I have an unlimited abundance of the material things I need.

I am a good person with a pure heart that wants to live my life in joy and love myself and others without condition.

I am comfortable with changes that occur in my life, they happen easily and I adapt to them well.

I have high self-esteem, I feel good about myself.

I look good and send out vibes of positive energy to all that I encounter.

I recognise that I create my world by the thoughts that I have and what I experience today is what I created yesterday.

I forgive myself and other people and recognise that we are all on a journey of learning.

I choose to see every experience whether positive or negative as an opportunity for learning.

Today I will listen to and understand my feelings and know that they are there for a reason.

The ultimate goal is to make a shift from your mind to your heart and intuition however, if you have been predominantly spending a huge portion of your time in your mind then affirmations are a great way to shift from negative to positive thought patterns.

Energy Healing

As I explained when I discussed energy on page 19 keeping the body's energy system clear and flowing freely is very important to creating mind, body, and spirit balance, most of the metaphysical and alternative practices that I am going to discuss focus on clearing and supporting the flow of energy through the body. The laying of hands over the body to channel positive healing energy and life force into the body's energetic system has been used for a long time by a range of different practitioners. Some energy healers are also skilled metaphysical practitioners such as psychic mediums who have the ability to communicate with other dimensional beings to support the guidance and direction of the energy healing.

Reiki

Reiki is different in that it uses pure universal or source consciousness energy that practitioners become attuned to by a Reiki Master. When healing with reiki both the giver and the recipient experience healing and there is no need for the healing to be directed in anyway as the healing is guided by source energy to where it is needed. Reiki can never do any harm to the recipient and there is now evidence that it can be very beneficial including reducing the negative side effects of chemotherapy and help with the regulation of the autonomic nervous system. If you feel that you need support with the clearing of your chakra and energetic system then consulting a trained reiki practitioner may be a good place to start. Again this is in conjunction with other methods I have discussed in the book. Also be guided by your intuition as to what feels right for you and when choosing a reiki practitioner, check their qualifications (and level) and whether or not you feel comfortable with the practitioner.

Crystals & Crystal Healing

When you fully realise that everything is energy, you begin to see things in a different light, in a different way, things take on a new perspective. You may have always been drawn to crystals or you may start to gravitate towards as a new thing, either way crystals can be a wonderful part of your life.

Crystals and the adornment of jewellery have been noted in history as long ago as 10,000 years BC and can be found in many different civilisations and cultures. They have also during that time been used not only for their aesthetic qualities but also for their healing properties. Crystals are also associated with spiritual development, psychic awareness and protection against negativity. Quartz crystals are capable of generating an electrical charge when placed under stress and it is quartz that is used to power watches. (Cassandra Eason 2010)

But what is it about crystals that makes them so useful? The majority of crystals have been grown in the earth or have come from a meteorite hitting the ground and there has been a lot of energy used in the creation of the crystal. That energy is unique to the individual crystal, even ones of the same type if they are grown in a different place in the world. It is the energy that is then stored in the crystal that transmits outwards and connects with our own body's energy system.

There are lots of books about crystals and they will tell you that certain crystals can be used for chakra clearing, or to help promote positivity or help a particular aliment. If you are new to crystals then these books can be a great guide to getting starting using crystals. They guide you to a particular crystal that can help you with whatever you are wanting support with, many explain the crystals origins and properties which can be really interesting too. Earlier in the book I discussed the body's energy systems and talked about chakras and the importance of keeping the energy flowing through the body to maintain good health and support mind, body, and spirit balance and crystals can help to clear negative energy and align and cleanse the chakras. Crystals I use for the cleansing and alignment of the 7 major chakras are:

Crown - Amethyst

Third Eye - Lapsis Lazuli

Throat - Blue Lace Agate

Heart - Emerald (raw state)

Solar Plexus - Sunstone

Sacral - Carnelian

Root or Base - Red Jasper

These are my own personal choices, for some lapis lazuli for example might be too strong for their third eye. Choosing crystals is a very personal thing and being self-aware, connecting to your intuition and allow that to guide you to the crystals that feel right for you will enhance their effectiveness and synergy with your own auric and energetic body.

The following process I use to do a crystal chakra clearing -

Having cleansed and charged your chakra crystals, make a time where you will not be disturbed and sit on the side of the bed, hold each crystal in turn and ask it to clear whichever chakra the crystal is for. Then lie down on the bed and place the crystals on each chakra starting at the root or base chakra and working your way up to the crown chakra.

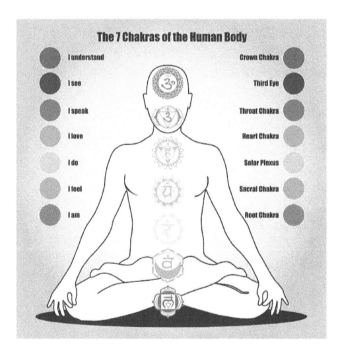

Colour version of the 7 major chakras of the human body can be found on my website at www.merlinpickston.com

Close your eyes and focus on your breathing for a few minutes and come into a state of light meditation, if thoughts come into your mind try not to get caught up in them, allow them to come and go and continue to focus on your breathing. Visualise a circle of bright white light surrounding your whole body as a circle of support. Chakras are on both sides of the body and meet within a central column of light that goes through the centre of your body emanating from the assemblage point. They spin clockwise to let energy out of the body and anticlockwise to bring energy into the body.

Starting at the root chakra, visualise a spinning wheel of light that goes through your entire body from front to back. Try to look into the wheel of light to see if it is clear or if they is any debris. Now connect to the crystal you placed on your root chakra and visualise the energy from the crystal going into the spinning wheel of light and clearing any debris or blockages.

Repeat the process for each of the 6 other chakras, if you find one feels blocked more you can spend more time with it. Once you have visually cleared each chakra then go back to focussing on your breathing. The whole process will probably take between 20 and 30 minutes. You can repeat this clearing again every couple of weeks if you feel you need to.

Other uses for crystals

Crystals can help with a wide range of issues, if you are having health issues crystals can support alongside other healing methods, they can also help with problems at work, blocking negative energy from others and more.

On a daily basis you may feel drawn to a particular crystal that you might like to wear or carry with you (within your energetic field) so if not around your neck as a pendant or in a crystal pouch then in a pocket. One lady I know carries the crystal in the top of her bra (in the cleavage). Again allow yourself to be guided to the crystal, your energetic body knows what it needs so you need to listen to what it is telling you.

Cleansing Crystals

Cleansing crystals is important to help them be fully connected to your personal energy, always ask or research what method of cleansing is best for the crystal you have chosen. There are a few methods you can use such as:

Water - placing the crystal under running water for a few seconds and then letting them dry naturally - note some crystals dissolve in water such as selenite so always check.

Clear quartz - this crystal can be used to cleanse and charge other crystals so place your crystals with a clear quartz (raw clear quartz is best) for 12 hours.

Salt - Leave crystals in sea salt for about 12 hours and then wipe with a soft cloth (kept for this use) - Note salt can be abrasive and softer crystals could get scratched.

Sound - the vibrational frequency of a Tibetan singing bowl is good for cleansing crystals, use the bowl over the crystals making sounds for about 2 minutes.

Sunlight - The power of direct sunlight can cleanse crystals very well, dawn to midday is the best time to do it. Note - some crystals may fade and lose their colour and some do not respond as well to the sun.

Moonlight - particularly on the full moon leaving crystals out in moonlight is a great way of cleansing crystals. Leaving them outdoors in direct moonlight is great or on a window sill.

I personally tend to use two methods, commonly water and moonlight, I find that the water cleanses and then the moonlight reenergises the crystal.

Programming Crystals

Setting an intention for what support or healing you want from the crystal is important. It maybe a good idea to write your intention down, and is often a good idea to be specific an example could be : I ask the crystal to use its energy to put a protective layer of light around me to stop negative energy come into my auric body.

Once cleansed hold the crystal in your dominant hand and ask the crystal what you would like its help with.

If you are using a crystal daily then regular cleansing needs to be done to reenergise the crystal.

There are also certain crystals that act as synergy stones that you can use to charge and increase the energy of other crystals, an example of one is peridot.

Crystal Healing

You can use crystals to support healing. At the beginning of my healing journey I used crystals to cleanse and start to clear my chakras, I did a clearing once a week. I used protection crystals daily to build resilience to negativity and then I used other crystals to help me with physical, mental, emotional and spiritual issues that I felt I needed to address. Like many metaphysical practices crystals support your overall process, they compliment, they synergistically work alongside your own conscious action to implement the changes you really want in your life.

There are some great books on crystals and crystal healing that guide you about what a crystal is and how it can help you and they are great for beginners and for general guidance. I tend to intuitively be guided to a crystal that is helpful for me at a particular time or moment. I ask the question about what it is I need help or support with and then I will either be drawn to it online or in a store or if I already own the crystal the image or name of it will come to me. You may also find that crystals find you and that is when the books are great to look up and see why!

Healing Baths

Water on its own is immensely healing. Think about how good you feel when just sitting in water whether that be in a bath, pool, lake or sea. The more natural the better, fresh lake water or sea water are great for us, indeed the salt in the sea can be very healing for both our physical and energetic bodies.

Chlorine the chemical found in most public swimming pools can trigger problems with breathing particularly those who are asthmatic. Chlorine also strips the natural oils out of the skin and hair and can cause irritation particularly for the eyes. If you are a regular swimmer in a public pool, protect your skin and hair by using products that clean the chlorine out, rinse the skin straight after swimming and use a good moisturiser. It is also advisable to drink plenty of water to clear out any chemical that may have been absorbed into the skin.

If you can swim in the sea do so as often as you can. If you do not live near a sea or ocean then using salts in your bath is a great as an alternative or as a supplement in winter months. Using epsom salts, magnesium flakes and essential oils in the bath water can benefit you in the following way:

- Relax and heal the muscles, particularly after exercising
- Cleanse negative energy out of the energetic body
- Absorb essential minerals into the skin that heals and cleanses

Again always keep well hydrated drinking plenty of water before and after the bath.

Sound Healing

Some of you may have heard of the Schumann resonance that measures the electromagnetic resonances that exist between the earth's surface and the ionosphere, also called Mother Earth's heartbeat, this was a very low frequency just short of 8Hz. The Schumann resonance was later connected to different brain waves that include Delta, Theta, Alpha, Beta and Gamma which are all occurring throughout the day in the brain during different activities from sleep to learning to creative pursuits. The Solfeggio frequencies refer to an ancient six tone scale that were incorporated into many sacred and ritual music; these six tones are also the notes A,C,D,E & G. Research in the 1970's revealed that these different frequencies showed that listening to them had a significant impact on the mind, body, and spirit balance and promoted healing in all 4 areas of the human being, mental, emotional, physical and spiritual. It was also demonstrated in the 1970's research that lower frequency music actually has a negative impact on mood, health and even DNA. There are a range of different frequencies and each can help with a variety of different things from overcoming depressive feelings, increasing your ability to feel love and pleasure, and clearing blocked chakras. Sound healing can also help you connect more deeply with your spiritual self to reducing physical pain and much more. There are a huge range of different music recordings broadcasting at different Hertz frequencies available on YouTube, check out which Hertz the recording is at and what the benefits of that particular frequency is. You can target the healing you want to do by choosing a different Hertz frequency to match. These can also be used as a part of your meditation practice.

Colour Healing

The use of colour to enhance life and health has been used since ancient times, it is used to heal all four of our 'bodies' physical, emotional, mental and spiritual. *Nina Ashby (2018)* explains the principles of colour healing. Each individual is made up of a combination of 'bodies' and each body vibrates at a different frequency that are connected to each other and work synergistically. Each 'body' responds differently to stimulation and as you affect or heal one body it has a knock on affect to the other 'bodies'. For example if you place a colour on the physical body it in turn affects your emotional, mental and spiritual bodies. Each colour has its own vibrational frequency (remember everything is energy), the energy frequency of the colour interacts with all four of your 'bodies' so depending on what colour you wear it will influence how you feel. The different colour energies also send out energetic messages to other people and how they interact with you. Nina Ashby (2018) goes on to discuss how 'each dis-ease has its own colour representation and by treating the dis-ease with the opposing colour at a vibrational level you can support healing.' She further explains that first one needs to identify the colour of the dis-ease or ailment, then its opposing colour and the colour of the chakra that the dis-ease is connected to so that the treatment can be made.

You will have seen earlier that the chakra system is colour coded and each chakra has a particular colour. If you are working on your root chakra to become more grounded then use a red crystal (like red jasper) and use a red colour such as a scarf or handkerchief (use natural material, silk has the highest vibration) on the chakra and this will enhance the healing and clearing of that chakra. You will probably find that as you are seeking a mind, body, and spirit balance you may well be drawn to the colours that you are lacking in or need in order to achieve the balance required. See the reference list for Nina Ashby's book and there are also a few others available from booksellers. Or search for a colour therapist in your area if this type of healing appeals to you.

PEMF Therapy

Pulsed Electro Magnetic Field is a completely non-invasive, pain-free therapy. It is the perfect fusion of digital touch screen technology & ancient wisdom that uses naturally occurring wave frequency, colour, light and crystalline energies. It re-activates the body's ability to self-heal by correcting imbalances in the body which manifest as physical illness. PEMF therapy is used to activate a humans ability to self-heal a wide range of conditions including children with asthma and eczema and also beneficial for adults with for instance Alzheimer's Disease, Anxiety and depression, arthritis, asthma & other lung and breathing disorders, and candida. It can also be used for chronic fatigue syndromes including ME, and fibromyalgia. It can also help with Influenza, Injuries, IBS, Joint pain, pain incl. back pain, PMT, Prolapsed disc, Repetitive Strain Injury, Sciatica, Skin complaints incl. eczema, psoriasis, burns, Stroke recovery, Ulcers and more.

Ananda Wellness website explains the 'PEMF therapy interacts with the mitochondria of your body and brain cells to boost their activity and get them to perform better. Mitochondria are the energy factories of the cells, when they are underperforming that is when stress, anxiety and pain as well as many other ailments can manifest. It is completely safe for almost everyone, has no side effects and is painless.'

Several examples of this type of therapy can be found in a range of native and ancient healing practices where a form of PEMF is used, traditionally, patients would lie down in the sun at midday, crystals placed on their body, enjoying the sunlight filter through the crystals. Crystalline energy, colour and light went deep into the tissues, organs and meridians of the body, stimulating the cells and healing any disease or imbalance. PEMF therapy is also used to address seasonal affective disorder, a direct result of insufficient light; chronic and bipolar depression; jaundice in newborn babies. NASA uses PEMF therapy to counteract the weightless environment in their astronauts.

I have personally received PEMF and received huge benefits from it including healing of shoulder and neck pain, stress relief, help with meditative visioning and the clearing and opening of my chakras. Please see my website www. merlinpickston.com for more details about how to obtain a machine of your own.

I discuss the assemblage point on page 21 and the PEMF can be used to adjust the AP back to its correct position. As discussed before AP can go out of alignment because of a number of different reasons and using PEMF following any of these events can help considerably with recovery.

Aromatherapy

Aromatherapy is fairly well known as a method of healing, it uses natural essential oils to improve the mind, body, and spirit balance. Aromatherapy has been used for thousands of years by a range of different cultures and some oils are also used in spiritual ceremonies. It works in two ways, through direct absorption into the skin and via the nose breathing in the healing scents. Using essential oils with candles or in electric defusers is very popular but you can also find essential oils in a range of products from bath salts to face creams. Different oils can be used to help a range of different ailments including headaches, improving digestion, managing pain, improving sleep, reducing stress and anxiety and to boost the bodies immune system. Aromatherapy is also used to help alleviate the side of effects of treatments such as chemotherapy and radiotherapy. If using essential oils on the skin it is best to test first and you should always use a carrier oil to dilute the essential oil into as they should not be used directly on the skin. Some people do get allergic reactions to some essential oils so test first and if in doubt as to whether you should use them consult a physician. Some people who are very sensitive to fragrances might want to avoid aromatherapy as it could well have an adverse reaction. There are some good books that can guide you on what to use and how to use essential oils. You can use a trial and error approach to see which work well for you, remembering that everyone's physiology is different. Alternatively you can use a certified aromatherapist who will look at your whole lifestyle and health situation and will advise which treatments will work best for you. I personally use oils in a defuser, in the bath and in some health and beauty products, I always find that natural is better and supports the mind, body, and spirit balance rather than a lot of the chemicals that are used in a lot of products.

Bowen Therapy

Bowen Therapy is gentle bodywork that addresses the white layer of the membrane between the skin and the muscles. The therapist rolls the thumbs and forefingers over areas of the body in order to stimulate nerve pathways in the body to allow message pathways to communicate. After each period of manipulation the therapist leaves the client to allow the communication to occur. The important element here is that the therapist facilitates self-healing and the time that the client is left alone allows the brain to form a response to the stimulation of the therapist. The body then is stimulated to begin healing the area that has been treated. There are a number of problems that this form of therapy can be used for including back and neck pain, sciatica, joint problems, sports injuries, autoimmune diseases, hormone imbalances and more.

Using Oracle & Tarot Cards

During your spiritual awakening you may find yourself drawn to tarot or oracle cards. First of all there are a lot of misconceptions about tarot cards in particular. I have met a number of people who have had a strong religious background who believe that using tarot cards is dangerous and invites evil spirits to the person who is reading them. Although both tarot and oracle cards should be used with respect, handled in a particular way and when reading them the right process followed, they are perfectly safe to use and can really help with listening to guidance from your intuition and true self.

Lots of people do not realise the difference between tarot and oracle cards; tarot cards are very traditional and are usually a set number of cards, commonly 78 and have a number of rules attached in the way that they are read. Tarot is most often used for divination and looking at themes in life, with guidance on direction. Unless someone has a natural gift it takes time to learn how to read tarot really well. There are a number of different themed tarot cards most are based on the original Rider Waite cards but you may feel drawn to a particular theme of card that you may find easier to interpret than others so go with your intuition when choosing them. Most people usually get used to a particular deck and stick with them, as regular use and familiarity with the deck improves ability in reading them.

Oracle cards on the other hand vary a lot, they are created by the author with a particular theme and there are lots of different themes available from mermaids to angels, moonology to butterflies and each theme may work on a different aspect of a life journey and spiritual awakening. The amount of cards in a deck can vary as can the theme of the deck. There are a couple of key points, firstly you can use more than one deck of oracle cards according to what you are currently working on and what feels right for you at the time, secondly you may grow out of a particular deck and feel drawn to a new one because of the advancements you have made. Oracle cards are usually easier to read than tarot and the guidance in them clearer and more straight forward.

Here are some basic guidance on keeping tarot and oracle cards:

- When you first open the cards hold them in your hands and bless them and allow your personal energy to go into the cards, then touch each card and hold it close to your heart
- Store the cards in a wooden box, card bag or piece of cloth
- Store with a quartz crystal
- If you read for others and they touch your cards or someone else uses your cards, when the reading is done use a pendulum to clear the other person's energy from the cards or use sound such as a Tibetan singing drum.

Reading Oracle Cards for Yourself

Once you have chosen the cards that you are drawn to and have blessed them and imbued them with your energy you can start to use them. Most decks come with a book telling you how to read them giving various layout options. Be guided by your intuition about the best way to read, you may want to just pick a card per day and use the cards visual and written meaning as a guide to what your intuition is wanting you to work on that day. Or you may choose to use several cards in a layout that will give you a wider message about what themes are going on for you and what to do to work with those themes. Oracle cards can be a great guide or even confirmation of something that you have been experiencing or feeling. Do not become obsessive about their meaning, use them as a tool to help raise your awareness and support your awakening journey.

Note about Divination

Whether you read your own tarot or oracle cards or get a reading with a professional psychic or medium it is important to remember a few key points about predicting future events. We all have free will choices and as such the path that we take through life although based on our life plan is affected by the choices we make. If a psychic told you that something was going to happen and then it didn't happen, it does not necessarily mean that the psychic was wrong, it could be that by having prior knowledge you then make a choice that leads you away from the event happening and changes the path that the psychic originally saw. The intention you have when using divination tools or seeking a professional in divination is important, do not use it just so you can feel better in the moment or try to find out if things are going to improve in your life because you are feeling low. Again this is about energy and the energy of the intention you are setting. Use the tools or information gained to help you to improve your life, as discussed before, take responsibility for yourself!

Working with Angels & Guides

Most people do not realise that we have a whole support network of angels and guides to help us on our human journey. Angels are commonly described in world religions but everyone's access to them is not so widely discussed. We all have at least one guardian angel who is with us our whole life and is there for protection and guidance, however there are also an array of angels and arch angels that can help with lots of different issues. You can learn more about the different angels and how they can help you. There are a couple of good writers who have published books that you can buy about angels including, Kyle Gray and Diana Cooper. In addition to angels everyone has a spirit guide who you choose before you incarnate and that guide knows your life plan and themes and sends you information psychically to help guide your path. They also work with angels to help create synchronicities in your life like meeting the right person at the right time or making you miss a bus because there will be an accident and so on. There are also lots of other guides that come and go according to what is happening in your life and they help you with different specialities. There are also ascended masters you can call on to help you, some are more well-known through mainstream religion than others, a couple of the well-known ones include Mother Mary, Mary Magdalene, Jesus, and Buddha.

I have found that one of the most important things you can do when you need help or support with healing or a problem or situation in your life is to actually ASK for help from your angels and guides, to say your own prayers. You will be amazed at how they shift and move into action to support you when you request their guidance and how you will see and feel the evidence of their intervention. It does not matter if you do not see or hear the guides, they are there. You need to connect to your intuition and your true self so that you can feel the guidance that you are being given. Sometimes support comes energetically when you will receive an angelic hug or love energy to help you through a difficult time.

Think about times when you have had so-called coincidences or synchronicities or when you have been through a difficult time, your angels and guides have been with you every time and will continue to do so. Now if you invoke their help you are drawing them closer to you and give them permission to help you even more, their divine guidance is so important for your awakening journey.

Homeopathy

Homeopathy is used by millions of people worldwide. Qualified homeopaths use a detailed and very holistic approach to diagnosis and recommendation of treatment taking into account a wide range of issues that an individual patient has, making the diagnosis and treatment specific to the individual. It is a natural form of medicine that is used with both acute issues and more long-term illnesses. The principle of homeopathy is that like cures like, taking a substance in small amounts will indeed cure the same symptoms it causes by stimulating the body's natural healing ability. Homeopathic remedies are created using a process of ongoing dilution and vigorous shaking, they contain small doses of plants and minerals and are strictly controlled. The remedies may come in the form of a cream, tablet, liquid or powder. The wonderful thing about homeopathy is that it has been used for hundreds of years and the remedies are gentle and there are rarely any side effects. You can buy homeopathic remedies over the counter in some pharmacies but I highly recommend finding a fully qualified homeopath who can fully assess and recommend remedies for you. A qualified homeopath will also be more than happy to work with your medical doctor and can also recommend other treatments that may support your healing. Research in your area and use your heart to guide you to the right homeopath for you.

There are many more holistic and alternative to medicine therapies that I have not talked about. The important point that I want to make is that during your awakening journey you may be drawn to different therapies at different times and whichever therapy you choose and use, do lots of research and trust your intuition to guide you to the right one and the right person. There is no right or wrong we are all unique just trust your heart to guide you. You may also find that a combination of therapies may suit you at different stages of your awakening and healing journey.

Guided Meditations

All 6 of the following guided meditations are available to buy as an Mp3 recording so that you can get the maximum benefit from them. Download them from my website at www.merlinpickston.com

Release a New You Guided Mediation

Find a comfortable place to sit, ensure that the temperature in the room is just right and you can sit without being disturbed. Once you are sitting comfortably, begin focussing on your breathing, in through the nose and out through the mouth, notice the rhythm of your chest and stomach going up and down, up and down, up and down, if any thoughts come notice them and let them go. Find an easy way of breathing again and turn your focus to your toes and your feet, send your breath all the way down to them and feel them relax, now move up to your legs feel the breath go to them and relax the muscles, they are soft and loose. Now relax your thighs and your hips and let go, your stomach and chest loosen and relax, your arms now are lying in a comfortable position and are totally relaxed. Your shoulders drop and relax as does your neck, any tension there just goes out with every exhale of breath. Now your face muscles, your jaw and forehead relax them all, let your tongue settle in your mouth.

Focus on your mind's eye, create circles of white light around you, in front of you is a door marked future me, walk towards the door and open it. Before you is a beautiful scene, you hear laughter, the scene is buzzing with positive energy. The people that you love and want in your life are there too, you see yourself, you are abundant in every way, you have all the love you deserve, you look amazing, you are wearing beautiful clothes, you are healthy and fit, your eyes are sparkling with joy and you have all the money you need. This is future you.

Take a step through the door and feel all of that abundant energy, feel the love, feel the joy, drink it all in and remember in your heart how it feels. Start walking towards future you until you are right next to future you. Step into future you, as you become one, feel what it feels like to BE future you. You are calm, peaceful, content, happy, joyous, at one with all around you, your heart is bursting with love for yourself and for the people around you, you feel the health of your body, its firmness and tone, your mind is calm and at one with your heart.

This is no longer future you, it is you now, you realise all of these wonderful feelings are available to you right now and as you walk back towards the door you carry those feelings with you, walking through the door those feelings stay with you and will be with you from this point onwards, and so it is.

When you are ready find yourself back in the room. You are now feeling relaxed, calm and refreshed and you still have those wonderful feelings with you. And so it is.

Find a Place of Inner Peace Guided Meditation

Find a comfortable place to sit, ensure that the temperature in the room is just right and you can sit without being disturbed. Once you are sitting comfortably focus on your breathing, in through the nose and out through the mouth, notice the rhythm of your chest and stomach going up and down, up and down, up and down. If any thoughts come, notice them and let them go.

Now find an easy way of breathing again and turn your focus to your toes and your feet and then send your breath all the way down to them and feel them relax, now moving up to your legs feel the breath go to them and relax the muscles, they are soft and loose. Now your thighs and hips, let go, let them relax, your stomach and chest loosen and relax, your arms now are lying in a comfortable position and are totally relaxed. Your shoulders drop and relax, as does your neck, any tension there just goes out with every exhale of breath. Now your face muscles, your jaw and forehead relax them all, let your tongue settle in your mouth.

Focus on your mind's eye and imagine that you are walking down a country lane, the ground is solid beneath your feet, the sun is shining and is warm on your face. You can hear bees buzzing and you can smell honeysuckle coming from the hedge rows.

You walk a little further and then come upon a gap in the hedge row, you take the turn and walk up a path in between fields of corn. As you walk you hear the corn rustle in the breeze and notice a field mouse on the end of an ear of corn. Walking a little further you reach the edge of a wood and enter a path that is mossy. The smell of ferns comes into your senses and you see squirrels running up and down trees.

You follow the path through the wood, there are bluebells scattered all around and their scent is sweet and pleasing. In the distance you see a female deer, she peers at you and then continues to eat foliage. Reaching the edge of the wood you come into a beautiful meadow that is filled with wildflowers, poppies and cornflowers give off bright red and blues colours. You walk further towards the centre of the meadow and find a comfortable place to sit down. The grass easily supports you and in the distance you hear the sound of a brook, the water babbling along, you notice more sounds, bees buzzing in and out of the flowers and birds singing and chirping in the trees.

This is a safe place, it is your sanctuary, your place of peace and calm, no one or nothing can hurt you here. You close your eyes and listen to the rhythm of your breathing and you feel perfect calm, perfect peace.

PAUSE FOR A 2 MINUTES OR SO

Remember this feeling of peace and calm, take note of this place and so whenever you need to, you can find this place again. You can visualise it and go there to drink in the peace and calm of your own sanctuary.

When you feel ready, get up from your place in the meadow and slowly walk back to the woods, walk through the woods, back through the corn field and along the country lane, and when you are ready, find yourself back in the room.

You are now feeling relaxed, calm and refreshed.

And so it is.

Healing the Inner Child Guided Meditation & Activation

Find a comfortable place to sit, ensure that the temperature in the room is just right and you can sit without being disturbed. Once you are sitting comfortably, close your eyes and focus on your breathing, in through the nose and out through the mouth, notice the rhythm of your chest and stomach going up and down, up and down, up and down. If any thoughts come, notice them and let them go. Now find an easy way of breathing again and turn your focus to your toes and your feet. Send your breath all the way down to them and feel them relax, now move up to your legs, feel the breath go to them and relax the muscles, they are soft and loose. Now your thighs and hips let go, let them relax, your stomach and chest loosen and relax, your arms now are lying in a comfortable position and are totally relaxed. Your shoulders drop and relax as does your neck, any tension there just goes out with every exhale of breath. Now your face muscles, your jaw and forehead relax them all, let your tongue settle in your mouth.

Focus on your mind's eye and surround yourself with circles of white light, and enter your inner world, this space allows for healing and full connection with your true self, here, you are fully protected and safe in this space. The ceremony has begun.

Breathe and begin to imagine that you are being transported back in time to your childhood. Tuning into the core of your inner child, the vibrant light, the joyful, playful, loving child, you may also notice feelings of fear or sadness or feelings of being unloved. Really tune into your inner child, now. Breathe and just be aware of what you see, hear and feel. Be aware of what your inner child wishes you to know, now.

You are reminded that your inner child is a child of the universe and has nothing but light, love, bliss, compassion, and understanding and this light is around you and within you. Breathe in the light, now.

The cosmic ray of healing love containing every colour of the spectrum, is being broadcast now and is customised to bring whatever nurturing, enchantment, and magick, that you need to refresh, revitalise, and reawaken the imagination of your inner child. The sense of well being, of knowing that you are provided for by the universe, and that all is well is coming forward now. This cosmic ray of healing love is activated, now.

Breathe in the cosmic ray of healing love, and then from the core of your being, notice any fear, feelings of abandonment, feelings of rejection, feelings of being unloved that are tied to past experiences. It is safe to do this.

These feelings are now elevated to the surface, are brought into the light of awareness, and released now into the cosmic ray of healing love.

The feeling of knowing that you are infinitely loved, of knowing that you are safe, feelings of well-being, of excitement, and of radiant joy, the high vibration of the true essence of your universal inner child downloads into your being, now.

Your inner child is a clear, vibrant light-being who is connected fully and completely to joy, love, and well-being and enters into this present time and space. The blueprint for your healed inner child downloads into your being, now

This blueprint begins to integrate qualities of playfulness, of self-love, of nurturing into your consciousness, now. You are able to draw upon all of these qualities now. Healing your present self begins by healing your past self, for all are connected and so the wounds of the past are ready to be released. Let them go, now. Whatever wounds or pain or struggles you experienced as a child are being healed now.

Be willing to let go of holding on to that pain, now. Be willing to replace that pain with the knowing that you are infinitely loved, now. The challenges of childhood, the challenges of life seek not to hold you down, seek not to break your spirit, but seek to provide you the contrast needed so that you are able to fully experience the light of the universe. Love is all around you. Well-being is all around you. The cosmic ray of healing love is all around you. Breathe them all in.

All this love and light goes through your body, refreshing each and every cell, pushing out at a cellular level, any beliefs, emotions, and toxic energy held within your being. Your energy may tense up for a moment before you release. Let it neutralise and go into the light. Release this now.

You are now able integrate fully the qualities of your inner child, bringing back your playful nature, your trust in the universe, your complete and total love, your divine imagination and well-being, self-love, and love for all.

And so it is.

Open your heart and let your love and gratitude and beauty flow out and go beyond yourself, rippling out love, joy, and happiness into the world. And so it is. Return your focus to your physical body, focusing within, and bring this uplifted frequency from the universe with you into this new cycle, into this new beginning. And so it is.

Plant seeds of intention about what you truly desire to create. Open your heart, be honest, love yourself, and go for it. And so it is.

When you are ready open your eyes and find yourself back in the room. You are now feeling relaxed, calm and refreshed. And so it is.

Balancing Feminine & Masculine Energies Guided Meditation

Find a comfortable place to sit, ensure that the temperature in the room is just right and you can sit without being disturbed. Once you are sitting comfortably focus on your breathing, in through the nose and out through the mouth, notice the rhythm of your chest and stomach going up and down, up and down, up and down. If any thoughts come, notice them and let them go. Find an easy way of breathing again and turn your focus to your toes and your feet and send your breath all the way down to them and feel them relax, now move up to your legs feel the breath go to them and relax the muscles, they are soft and loose. Now your thighs and hips let go, let them relax, your stomach and chest loosen and relax, your arms now are lying in a comfortable position and are totally relaxed. Your shoulders drop and relax as does your neck, any tension there just goes out with every exhale of breath. Now your face muscles, your jaw and forehead relax them both, let your tongue settle in your mouth.

Focus on your mind's eye and surround yourself with a circle of pink light and a circle of blue light and enter your inner world, this space allows for healing and full connection with your true self, the ceremony has begun.

Take three deep breaths slowly in and out and move your awareness from your head to your heart; you are sitting on a bench in a beautiful garden, you take in the smell of roses and the scent of jasmine, the garden is vast with a huge lawn and beds of flowers around the edges. In the centre, set upon a podium is a circular arbour and set in the middle of the arbour is a table. You cannot see what is on the table but your curiosity is piqued and you get up from the bench and walk towards the podium.

You reach the bottom of the steps of the podium and start walking up, when you reach the top of the steps you see in front of you a table and in the centre of the table is a set of beautiful brass scales, you take a moment to appreciate the workmanship in the scales. Looking at the pans of the scales you see the one on the left represents your feminine side and the one on the right represents your masculine side. Look carefully and notice in which direction the pans of the scales are tipped, more to the left, feminine or the right, masculine?

Go deep within yourself to identify the divine masculine and divine feminine traits that you feel you need to bring forth and embody. The divine feminine traits will be pastel in colour, they will be soft, flowing and sweet smelling; the divine masculine traits will have primary colours of different shades, they will be firm, have straight lines, have the scent of pine and be rough to the touch.

Back on the pagoda you begin to notice flower petals floating towards you from the left side of the garden, they are pretty pastel colours. One floats down onto your hand, written on it is the word love, you place this onto the left pan of the scales, another petal floats onto your hand it has the word compassion written on it and again you place this onto the left side of the scales. One by one pastel petals fall onto your hand with the different qualities of divine feminine energy including the traits that you brought forth before, and each one you place onto the left pan of the scales.

Now you notice flower petals coming from the right side of the garden, they are all bold primary colours, a red petal lands in your right hand and has the word strength written on it, you go and place the petal onto the right pan of the scales. Another petal floats down it is a deep blue colour and lands onto your right hand, it has the word confidence written on it, you take the petal and place it onto the right pan of the scales. One by one primary coloured petals fall onto your hand with the different qualities of divine masculine energy including the traits you brought forth earlier, and each one you place onto the right pan of the scales.

You look at the scales and now see that they are balanced, you look into the pan of the divine feminine qualities and all of the petals have turned into a thick liquid and then rising out of the liquid you see the form of a beautiful woman who stands to the left of the table where the scales sit. You now look into the pan of the divine masculine qualities and all of the petals have also turned into a thick liquid and then rising out of the liquid you see the form of a handsome man who stands to the right of the table where the scales sit.

The two people represent the two parts of you, in the air you see floating an infinity symbol and one end of the symbol goes around the wrist of the man and the other around the wrist of the woman, the symbol binds the masculine and feminine traits together as a whole, they are now one.

The man who represents the masculine within you turns into water, at the same time the woman who represents the feminine within you turns to air. The air spins around the water bringing it up into a whirlpool and the whirlpool goes towards your heart chakra, it then pours into your heart chakra and goes down into your solar plexus and sacral chakras. The infinity sign that binds them goes through your third eye chakra. The balanced masculine and feminine aspects of you are now fully integrated into your mind, body, and spirit.

Sitting in the arbour you feel a sense of peace, of oneness with yourself, you feel whole, balanced and at peace.

And so it is.

Now return your focus to your physical body, focusing within, bring with you the sense of balance, oneness and peace forward into a new beginning as a person with fully balanced divine feminine and divine masculine qualities.

When you are ready find yourself back in the room. You are now feeling relaxed, calm and refreshed

And so it is.

Finding your True Self Guided Mediation

Find a comfortable place to sit, ensure that the temperature in the room is just right and you can sit without being disturbed. Once you are sitting comfortably focus on your breathing, in through the nose and out through the mouth, notice the rhythm of your chest and stomach going up and down, up and down, up and down, if any thoughts come, notice them and let them go. Find an easy way of breathing again and turn your focus to your toes and your feet and send your breath all the way down to them and feel them relax, now move up to your legs feel the breath go to them and relax the muscles, they are soft and loose. Now your thighs and hips let go, let them relax, your stomach and chest loosen and relax, your arms now are lying in a comfortable position and are totally relaxed. Your shoulders drop and relax, as does your neck, any tension there just goes out with every exhale of breath. Now your face muscles, your jaw and forehead relax them both and let your tongue settle in your mouth.

Focus on your mind's eye and surround yourself with circles of white light and enter your inner world, this space allows for healing and full connection with your true self, the ceremony has begun.

You are walking along a beautiful sandy beach, the sand is nearly white and the aquamarine sea laps onto your bare feet. You can see a few wisps of clouds in the bright azure sky and palm trees swish in a light breeze. You hear the sounds of dolphin clicks and whale song coming from the ocean. As you walk, you see a group of people sitting on the beach talking, as you get closer to them you feel as if they are very familiar to you. They see you and smile and wave beckoning you to come and join them.

You approach the group and the first person steps up and says hello to you. They are smartly dressed but their face is wrinkled, they have bags under their eyes, their hair is unkept and they look very tired. They introduce themselves and as they speak their voice sounds hollow, 'I am your outward persona, I am the person that you let other people in the world see, I am your false self, your critical self.' They step back and a couple step forward, they are holding hands and standing very close to each other, the man is very handsome with a kind, strong smile and the woman is beautiful with sparkling eyes and a deep loving gaze, they speak as one, 'we are the masculine and feminine principles within you, our divine qualities bring you balance and we harness your creativity and manifesting abilities, we bring you harmony'

They step back and a child runs forward and hugs your legs, they look up at you with bright eyes and beautiful innocence, they ask you if you can go play with them, you nod and smile and take their hand, they sit in the sand and begin to build a sand castle, you start to use a spade and scoop sand into a bucket and pass it to the child who is creating a large castle. Methodically you work together humming songs and laughing as you build. As the child places the last piece of the sand castle they giggle and whoop and then they ask you 'what do you see at the gates of the castle?' You look at the gates and are surprised to see someone standing guard at the gates. The outward persona and the couple join you and the child, and then the child mischievously says, 'Shall we go to the castle?' You all say, 'Yes!' You then join hands and are instantly transported to the castle gates.

You step forward towards the gates and see a very tall person at least 2 metres tall standing there, they look down on you and say,'You cannot enter it is not safe inside'. You ask them ' why, what is inside?' They tell you 'Someone you have not seen for a very long time, seeing them, trusting them may not be safe for you, best go back now'

You ask them, 'Who are you?' They respond ' I am your ego, I am here to protect you!' You thank them for protecting you but insist that you really want to go inside the castle; all of a sudden your ego shrinks to your size and looks you in the eye, they say'If you insist but I will be right behind you, just in case'

The gates of the castle open and all the aspects of you that you have met so far walk through into a huge hall way, there is a huge stone staircase coming down on the left hand side of the grand hall and on the right are huge stone lions on either side of a wooden doorway. Hanging from the ceiling is a huge crystal chandelier that sparkles with light. You hear someone coming along the upstairs landing and see them start to walk down the stairs. You look up at them and see the most beautiful person, they carry themselves with grace and you can see their aura glowing light rainbow colours around them. You see light coming from their heart and feel the love that they are sending you pouring into your body. They reach the bottom of the stairs and smile looking deeply into your eyes, you see that it is your face in front of you, they take your hand and lead you towards the two wooden doors on the opposite side of the room.

The wooden doors open and you look out into a beautiful courtyard garden, walking to a bench on the right side of the garden you sit and ask, 'who are you?' They answer, 'I am your true self, the light of your divine being, who you really are, I have waited so long to finally meet you, although I have always been with you, I have not been able to reach you before.'

Your true self speaks 'I love you, I am your guide, your mentor, your confidant, I will provide you with all these things and more which you will feel as your intuition, or an idea that comes to you, I am the voice of your heart, all you have to do is listen and I am there.'

Your true self places their hand on your heart chakra and opens the door of your heart, you feel deep love and joy within you and then your true self merges with you.

All of the other aspects of you come into the garden, and one by one they merge into you as well and you all become one. With renewed purpose and a sense of finally being whole you walk back out into the grand hall and out of the gates of the castle.

Now back on the beach you look out across the ocean once again hearing the sounds of dolphins and whales and with a deep sense of inner peace, you sit on the sand soaking up the rays of the warm sun.

Now return your focus to your physical body, focusing within, bring with you the knowledge that you true divine self is with you ALWAYS.

When you are ready find yourself back in the room. You are now feeling relaxed, calm and refreshed.

And so it is.

Meditation to Align to your True Life Purpose

Before you start this mediation write your date of birth down on a piece of paper and have it in front of you, if you know the day of the week and time include that also. Example: Tuesday 21st October 1986, 13.30.

Find a comfortable place to sit, ensure that the temperature in the room is just right and you can sit without being disturbed. Once you are sitting comfortably focus on your breathing, in through the nose and out through the mouth, notice the rhythm of your chest and stomach going up and down, up and down, up and down, if any thoughts come, notice them and let them go. Find an easy way of breathing again and turn your focus to your toes and your feet and send your breath all the way down to them and feel them relax, now move up to your legs feel the breath go to them and relax the muscles, they are soft and loose. Now your thighs and hips let go, let them relax, your stomach and chest loosen and relax, your arms now are lying in a comfortable position and are totally relaxed. Your shoulders drop and relax, as does your neck, any tension there just goes out with every exhale of breath. Now your face muscles, your jaw and forehead relax them both and let your tongue settle in your mouth.

Focus on your mind's eye and surround yourself with circles of white light and enter your inner world, this space allows for healing and full connection with your true self, the ceremony has begun.

You are floating on a cloud. You can see the earth beneath you and high up in the sky you see the stars. As you look around you see the different constellations, you feel drawn to a particular constellation, the one in which you were born in. The cloud you are on goes higher and higher, just as you reach the edge of the atmosphere a wave of light lifts you up and sweeps you along towards your constellation of birth.

As you arrive at your constellation you see its formation and are drawn to one star in particular. The energy wave takes you there and you see a planet, there is a familiarity deep within you, you are drawn to the planet and as you get closer the wave of light takes you to the planet. Floating through the atmosphere into the sky, you notice the differences between here and earth and take a moment to observe them all.

In the distance you see a building, you are drawn closer to it and see that it is a temple. As you approach it you see that the temple is made of pure white marble and is octagonal in shape and has steps from the ground that lead up to the temple gates.

Now at the temple you walk up the steps and through the gates, inside is very bright filled with pure light, it takes you a few moments to adjust and then you see a number of doors leading off a hallway. You are drawn to the door in the North and walk towards it. The huge door has large brass handles shaped in the star sign of your birth, you open the door and step into the room. You see a huge library with books going from floor to ceiling all around the room. You see a sliding ladder and you go up to it, on the ladder you see a keyboard, you enter your birth date in full. The ladder then moves around the room and stops at a space to the far west of the room, you walk over to it and climb the ladder and see a book sticking out from the shelf, you pick the book up, go down the ladder and take it to a table in the centre of the room.

You open the book and the words, pictures and numbers rise up from the page and swirl about the room. Each one is lite up, you see your exact date and time of birth, you see pictures of significant events in your life, words that represent your life path and purpose.

Your spirit guide and guardian angel appear either side of you and they step forward and each of them begin to open your chakras one by one. You feel the energy in your chakras go faster and vibrate, you feel a tingling sensation throughout your whole body and then the words, pictures and numbers that are floating in the room begin to pour into your crown chakra, they then go down and each word, picture and number settles into the chakra that it represents.

Once this imprint has been placed into your energetic system you feel a strong sense of alignment, a new feeling of direction in your life, a positive vibe that you know exactly where you want to go and what you want to do and that you will receive help in achieving that, you feel that your true life purpose is clear.

Your spirit guide and guardian angel bless you and open a door way and tell you to walk through it. You walk through and find yourself back in your home.

Now return your focus to your physical body, focusing within, bring with you the positive energy, focus and determination that the alignment with your life purpose has brought you.

When you are ready find yourself back in the room. You are now feeling relaxed, calm and refreshed.

And so it is.

AWAKENING TO THE MAGICK IN YOUR LIFE

As you really begin to awaken and make changes to your life practically and behaviourally there are a number of things that happen to you on all four levels of your being, physically, emotionally, mentally, and spiritually. As you awaken you will find that you see life in a really different way, you appreciate the things you have and you see the magick within and around you and how you can attract even more of that magick into your life.

As I discussed in the introduction having a mentor or someone to talk to about these changes is really important. I am going to discuss how some of these changes may manifest in your life and give you some tips on how to deal with them. Remember that each journey is unique and individual so these are guidelines, you may get some, all or none of these things but with my own personal experience and from my doctorate research I feel that you are most likely to get some of the symptoms that I describe in the next section.

How to manage changes that occur during awakening & self-discovery

Change is challenging for the majority of human beings, we like what we know, we feel comfortable with it and when something new comes along our ego is not a fan! The more that you connect with your heart and trust your intuition the less scary change becomes. It is good to recognise that other people also have an issue with change and when you start to change your behaviour you may find that you do not always get the reaction you would hope for from friends, family and colleagues. Working with clients and speaking with friends who have or are going through behavioural change and awakening they have had a number of different reactions from the people around them including:

- Being accused of being weird, strange and odd
- Saying that the change is bad and that you are not a nice person
- Saying they don't know you anymore and you should stop and go back to the person you were before

All of these negative comments are all about the other person and these are their issues and not about you at all. Do not get discouraged by negative comments that you may receive from the people around you. The best way of dealing with any of these comments is to lovingly thank them for their opinion and tell them how you feel about them however you are happy with the changes that you have made for yourself and intend to continue with them and that you hope that they will come to see the changes in you as positively as you do. It can be hard when the people you love the most find it hard to deal with the changes that you are making in your life, but it is important to remember that it is your life and you need to stay true to yourself and be authentic. If you do not then unhappiness and dissatisfaction will be a part of your life and these types of so called sacrifices for other people end up causing issues within relationships. If people truly love you they will love the true you that you are unveiling as part of your discovery and awakening journey.

You will hopefully have some people you know who see and recognise good change in you and get some great comments too.

The following are symptoms that you may experience during your awakening journey:

Physical Symptoms

- A change in sleep pattern
- Changes or fluctuation in body weight
- Tingling in the crown of the head
- Changes in eating patterns and developing food intolerances
- Increased sensitivity of the senses
- Physical pain or symptoms some include headaches, body pain, racing heart, cramps, chest tightness, feeling unusually hot or cold, stomach upset, flu-like symptoms, skin eruptions. All of these are temporary, rest when required and listen to your body. Try to avoid using chemical medications to treat these symptoms
- Faster hair and nail growth
- Left brain fogginess which is part of the balancing of masculine and feminine energies
- Dizziness - this can be caused by a lack of grounding and connecting to Mother Earth will help this using the grounding exercise earlier in the book

Emotions & Feelings

- Sudden waves of emotion
- Waves of high levels of energy and then exhaustion
- Emotional confusion
- Wanting to be alone
- Impatience
- Feeling you are different to other people
- Increased intuition
- Feeling closer to animals and nature
- Feeling you want to find your soul mate
- Seeing a person's true form good or bad
- Feeling that there are things in your life that you need to end or complete and then move on

Spiritual

- Vivid dreams, ones that you can remember all of the details of, ones that include all of the senses and very vivid colours
- Perception that time is accelerating
- A sense that something big is going to happen
- A deeper need for meaning and purpose in your life
- Teachers appear in your life just when you need them
- A deep sense that you have found your spiritual path
- A sense of invisible presences around you that seem just out of reach
- A greater connection to nature and the earth
- Ideas flow more easily, you think about something and then it happens or a synchronicity occurs in your life towards that goal, thought, or intention
- Memories surface from the past or from past or parallel lives that need to be allowed to flow through you
- You feel more like you are living your life's purpose
- You get intuitive communication from your guides, angels and other divine beings

Handling these symptoms can feel overwhelming and self-care is vital in order to ensure that you manage them in a positive way. Doing that around your daily life can be a challenge and you may find that you need to let go of some of the things that you do and get support from your partner and children or friends to ensure that you get enough time for yourself. If you need extra sleep then rest, if you need to change what you are eating then make those changes, constantly listening to what your internal self is telling you and reacting on it is really important in managing how you are during your awakening journey. You may feel guided to make bigger decisions about careers, relationships and where you live that are more long term. Ultimately you need to do what is best for you, each step that you take illuminates the way for the step after that and if you truly listen to your heart, your true self, then you will find that the steps become easier. If you however allow your fearful ego to get in the way then you will have a more difficult time. Even if you do fall prey to the ego's fear being self-aware and using the exercises in this book to help you to come back to your true self will ensure that you do not go off track for long.

Sleep, Dreams & Dream Interpretation

We all dream, but people often report that they do not remember their dreams. This may be because of their particular sleep pattern or because they have an overactive mind. Once you start to become more mindful during waking hours, begin the process of coming off autopilot and being more present, you can begin to train your mind to be calmer and less active; you are also more likely to remember your dreams. You will also find it much easier to actually get to sleep when you go to bed. There are exceptions of course, a person on permanent autopilot may still remember their dreams, it all depends on what their subconscious mind is dealing with and processing. Sleep and dreaming are unique to the individual and are often influenced by things like, childhood experiences, any trauma associated with sleeping, work and work patterns, how tired the physical body is and so on. Additionally sleep patterns change according to what is happening in your life and the stage of life you are in. Whether you sleep well or not there are lots of things that you can do to increase the likelihood that you get a restful night's sleep. People who do sleep do not necessarily get restful night and can often wake feeling as tired as they did before going to sleep. Here are a few suggestions to help with getting restful sleep:

- Spend a few times a day actively being 'present' and not on autopilot
- Do not eat too close to bedtime
- If you are prone to waking to go to the toilet in the night take you last drink a good hour before bed
- Do any exercise a good couple of hours before bedtime
- Don't watch anything too exciting too close to bedtime
- Do not use mobile phones or tablets in bed (blue light from them can cause you to stay awake)
- Create a sanctuary in your bedroom, it should be calming, soothing and a place that is conducive to sleep, TV's in bedrooms are not always a good idea
- Take a bath before bed (use the salts as discussed on page 120)
- Meditate before going to bed
- If you are prone to lying in bed worrying or thinking about what you need to do or reflecting on the day, spend time before bed writing a list of things to do, or journal about your day or write a list of your worries

- Another important factor is to make sure that your bed and mattress is the right one for you so that you are comfortable enough to sleep well
- If you still struggle to sleep you could use a herbal supplement to aid sleep such as valerian on a temporary basis but always consult a healthcare professional to make sure this is right for you and what dose would be suitable

During a spiritual awakening it is particularly important to take note of any significant dreams that you remember. I highly suggest having a note pad and pen by your bed to take notes of dreams that you have as soon as you wake up so that you have it as a reference as we often forget details of the dreams or forget them all together. Commonly we wake after a particularly significant dream following a period of REM (rapid eye movement) sleep which most people enter into several times during a sleep period. These dreams are the ones to take notice of, particularly if they are sequential and not all mixed up and that flow naturally (however bizarre or odd).

As you awaken you will find that you begin to see and feel experiences in a different way and this is the same for dreaming and dreams. Our subconscious mind and our true self work together to support the process of healing old psychological, mental, and emotional wounds and these can come forth in dreams. These traumas could be from fairly recent times or from childhood or many years ago. You may not dream of the actual event but things related to that event and it may be mixed with things in your current life. Writing these dreams down and spending a little time analysing them or discussing them with a trusted friend or mentor can help with your healing process and letting go of old trauma.

Fears can also manifest in dreams, if you are afraid of something happening to someone you love for example this may come in a dream but it does not mean that the dream is prophetic and is going to happen but rather is letting you know how deeply that fear is affecting you. Working on letting go of the fear is the answer to preventing you having the dream again.

We can also have recurring dreams and these are often linked to one of two things or both, firstly it could be unresolved conflict that is still in play in your life or secondly it could be linked to a life theme or lesson that you have not yet learned. Life will put opportunities in place for you to learn the lesson and the dreams are a way of reminding you that it still needs to learned. An example of this could be, people taking advantage of your kindness, unless you learn to say no or set suitable boundaries with people (which is the lesson) then people will continue to take advantage of your kindness. Your dream could be about your feelings of anger, disappointment and frustration and in the dream you may tell the people who take advantage of you that it is not acceptable thus doing in the dream what you need to do in life.

You may also have dreams about a particular person that you do not know in this lifetime and they may appear many times in dreams. This could be one of your guides sending you messages in your dreams to help you.

What can also happen (and does with me on a very regular basis) is that you may dream of past or parallel lives and you may dream about a life that is completely different from your current one. These dreams come to your conscious mind for a reason and it is good to analyse them and see if you can identify any connections to your current life situation, examples could include :

- A similar situation that you are dealing with in your current life and the knowledge learned from the previous life can help you in the now
- A trauma that occurred in a past or parallel life may be causing issues for you in your current life and understanding what happened to you before can help you to resolve the problem or bring deeper understanding
- Dreams of other lives can also give you a greater feeling of who you are in the wider sense, the realisation that your life and your true self is greater than your current experiences

Whatever form your dreams take, and they are all helpful in your awakening journey, it is good to take note of them and analyse them but do not become obsessive about them simply use them as further messages from your subconscious mind and your true self to help you on your journey.

Awareness of Others

There are a number of different behaviour patterns that can be observed in people. It is important to identify some of these because you may not be aware that you are doing these things yourself, or you maybe experiencing them in one of your relationships and as a result the behaviour is affecting your day to day life or the nature of your relationship. They may also be linked to codependency, self-sabotage and narcissism discussed earlier in the book. Some of the behaviours include :

Victim - I am sure everyone knows a person that is always having a drama, if there is an illness going around they get it, if there's a scam they fall prey to it, it's their partner that cheats or their best friend that lies about them and so on. In most cases victims do not want to be helped, they like being the victim and speak about their woes to get attention and any energy spent listening to them and trying to help them will be in vain and will simply drain your energy and leave you feeling depleted.

Manipulators and Controllers - These individuals border on obsession when it comes to getting what they think they want, they will lie, cheat, twist truth, plant information and gossip to get what they want. Being fully aware of these types of people in your life can help you to ideally avoid them or if they are family that you cannot avoid then at least you can manage their behaviour so that you do not fall prey to their manipulation. Change is also really difficult for them and they will do all they can to stop, halt, put a spanner in the works of change unless it is something that they want to happen. Fear is their primary driver and if you hope to deal with someone like this then dealing with their fear would be a good place to start.

Rescuers - These people (and this could also be you) want to save people, they see pain and hurt and jump to the aid of others, yes they can be kind and caring but they often do this to fulfil a need or lack within themselves, helping others makes them feel good and they often help others to the detriment of themselves. Additionally they put up with and accept poor behaviour from others as a result of their deep desire to rescue them.

Working Towards Successful Relationships

Do you feel that relationships are difficult or hard? Do you find that people are hard to understand? This is often quite common.

From a metaphysical perspective the more incarnations a person has had the more life experiences they have gone through and so their ability to understand and empathise with another person is greater than a soul that has had fewer multiple life experiences.

A key principle here is that you cannot change other people, you cannot change their behaviour _you can only change your own behaviour_. The key to successful relationships is to work on yourself, work on your own behaviour, and make changes to yourself. Use the 7 Pillars of Personal Change, particularly self-awareness and observation (Pillar 1 and 2) when you are interacting with others, be aware of what you are thinking and feeling during your interactions. Remember that you are giving and receiving psychic information during your interactions with other people, being present and mindful will enable you to really hone in on what you are really receiving, seeing and hearing during your communications with other people. If you are not present, not mindful, you will be going into your emotional storehouse and past experiences and this will impact the way in which you react during your social exchanges.

Empathy is an important skill when managing your relationships and the ability to be able to see things from other people's perspective vitally important. If we have experienced something similar to another person then we use that in how we interact with that person, it can make it easier because we have a point of reference to use in how we communicate. That said it is also common for people to use their own experience of a situation to communicate to others in a negative way by making assumptions about what the other person is going through. The key here is to really LISTEN, WATCH and FEEL, what is that person actually saying to you, what is their body language and what feelings are you getting from the psychic information they are sending you.

Things become more difficult if we do not have that point of reference, many people then view or observe another person's behaviour and it feels alien to them. We then either do not understand, react in a way that shows our lack of understanding through emotions such as frustration and anger or indifference. These emotions are based on how the other person's behaviour is affecting us and how we feel as a result.

It is pertinent to mention that people communicate in different ways, verbal communication and being open about how they feel, expressing what they actually want and need may not be easy for some people. They may express these things negatively through poor behaviour such as anger, being silent, saying things that are not true, 'I'm fine' is a good example. However the information they are sending to you through body language and psychic information will be honest as this is coming from the heart rather than the ego. Watching and feeling for what the person is really trying to express is very important. Many of us do that automatically without realising what we are doing but often this is not consistent and is ALWAYS reliant on whether or not we are present (being mindful) or whether we are on autopilot.

Using the zooming out exercise on page 94 is good to use in your interactions, to really help you understand what is happening and can help you see things from another person's perspective.

As a society we have been programmed that if we work on ourselves, do things for ourselves, put ourselves first then we are being selfish and so we are not being a good person. The reality of the situation is that putting ourselves first makes us a much more rounded person, a happier person, and a much better person to be with. We are then far more able to manage and be with others in a very positive way, people want to be around us and it makes relationships much easier. Many people do lots of wonderful things for others, they give all the time, go out of their way, be a good friend and a good listener and that is wonderful however it is often done to make them feel that they are a good person, the busier they are, the more they do, the better they then feel about themselves however this is a bit like borrowing money from the bank and having to pay interest on it at some point it comes back to bite you. This can be in the form of a friend taking you for granted, draining your energy to make them feel better, or your physical self getting so worn out that you are ill. Self-care and self-love is what leads to good relationships and part of that is knowing how and when to do the following:

- Walk away from people - if someone treats you poorly, does not respect you, is abusive, does not show you the love you deserve then walking away from them is absolutely the thing to do, it is not easy I know but they only way and if that person happens to be your spouse or mother, or father then so be it. Even if it is for a short period of time to give space and to come back to them later and set clear boundaries for the future.
- Saying no - This is one that many people find hard to do, they end up finding themselves doing all sorts of things for other people that they do not really want to do.They give up their own time and energy all for helping others. Balance is the key word here, its great helping people as long as it is not to your own detriment and as long as other people do not take you for granted. Saying no to such people is a big step in taking back your own power rather than giving it away to others. Be aware that people pleasing is a form of codependency.

- Balance of giving and receiving - This leads on from saying no, lots of people feel okay to give, they will give very easily, indeed give away their self and their power but struggle with receiving. This is because of a lack of worthiness, lack of self-esteem and so they do not feel they deserve good things coming their way. Lots of people reject offers of help, support, gifts etc for this very reason. If this is you, next time someone offers, say YES! Balance is the key.
- As you continue your awakening journey you will find that how you react and feel towards others will change and at the beginning it will be a surprise, you may say to yourself,'where did that come from.' The further you go along your journey the more you will shift from reaction to consideration into forming a loving calm response to others. Learning how to make that transition will come to you particularly as you work through some of the exercises and activities in this book. The more present you become, the more you focus on creating a mind, body, and spirit balance and the more that you work towards being your true self all of the time the more that you will be able to respond to others in the best way possible, from a loving perspective. This does not mean that you back down, this could mean that you are assertive and stand up for yourself but from a position of love instead of a negative emotion.
- You will find that relationships will also change, the ones you currently have will be different, you may well lose people as you outgrow them and that is okay, love them and let them go. You will also find that new people are brought into your life who will help you with your awakening journey, some may stay for a short while to help with a particular issue or problem and others will be with you long term. Enjoying, learning, and being with these people

during those times is important so that you can bring forth the growth that you need at the right stage of your awakening journey. When meeting new people it is important not to go back into old behaviour patterns when establishing relationships, setting boundaries, seeing things from others perspective, sitting in your own personal power and having high levels of self-awareness and empathy are important behaviours to adopt.

Children & Parenting

Once you have done some work with your inner child you may want to use your new knowledge about the wounding that you received as a child to evaluate how you parent your own child or children. You should not beat yourself up about any past mistakes but look to see how you can change your interactions with your child or children. The emotional wounding of a child is part of the process of growing, the innocence of children does not allow them to know and understand the subtleties of complex human interactions and life and so they become wounded when they do not realise what is happening. For example, you get home from work late, you have had a terrible day at work and you come home and your child wants to show you something or share something with you, you are not in the mood and all you want to do is sit down and have a glass of wine, you dismiss the child saying you'll see later and do it in a grumpy way. The child does not know that you are tired, have had a bad day or why you are late and why they are being dismissed grumpily. They may see and feel as if they are being rejected, not loved, not safe. If this happens enough times it becomes an emotional wound and the child will carry that feeling with them. If this is then reinforced by other behaviour by their parent or parents then it can become a deeper problem. Minimising the wounding they experience whilst preparing them for life is deeply important. When we think about what many western children in particular need we often think and see material things and preparing them for life we see education for example but there are the core things that children need that are sometimes overlooked and overcomplicated and they include:

- Feeling unconditionally loved - If love is made conditional (if they are naughty then they are not loved or if they don't do their chores they are not loved, or if everything that the parent does for them is thrown back in their face) then the child will behave in a controlling way. They will do all they can to control the outcomes of situations to make them feel loved. This is where attention seeking behaviour can begin.
- Feeling safe - safety that they will not be hurt, have their own space, that things will not be taken away from them, that they will be fed and given all their basic needs without anything being withheld, that they are protected by their caregivers or parents
- That there is no risk of them being abandoned, lost or left behind, they need a sense of security that caregivers and parents will also be there for them

Trauma can also be experienced during pregnancy, we know that the foetus responds to music being played and indeed are sensitive to the energy that their mother is subjecting them to, if their mother is involved in arguments and traumatic situations then the child will be born with that wounding already in place.

Additionally you could also think about what you have learnt from this book and perhaps other metaphysical teachings, how can you translate these to help the way in which you parent your child or children? How amazing would it be if your child knew how to be mindful, was not judgemental of others or themselves, learnt how to meditate, had good self-esteem and self-love, ate healthfully, exercised regularly, and was on they way to becoming their true self and not creating a persona that they think they should be because of societal pressure and brainwashing? You may also want to reflect on whether or not you want to give your child or children any type of vaccine or whether you want to allow their fully effective immune systems to develop naturally.

The knowledge from this book may also help you to realise things about your child or children, understand them better and help you to help them. For example your child may come out with wisdom beyond their years or show a wonderful amount of compassion or love or be drawn to metaphysical things, lots of children love crystals for example. This could be that they have reincarnated many times in past or parallel lives and this wisdom comes from their other life experiences. They may say that they have an 'imaginary friend' do not dismiss this it is quite possible that they are indeed seeing a guide or friend that is helping them in their early years. Be inquisitive, ask them questions about their friend and do not make them feel that they anything is wrong with them. Additionally if they are naturally psychic then if encouraged they will not 'grow out' of it.

Children & Generations

As social situations have changed over the decades since the second world war so have the children that have been born each decade. Commonly known theories about the generations and how the social and economic situations have influenced them such as generation x, y and z and millennials are used significantly in business and marketing and in social and psychological analysis but metaphysically there is also another aspect that is not discussed. That is the fact that the global awakening and shift in consciousness of the earth and humankind has been foreseen by many different prophets in ancient and native cultures across the world and because of that children have been born in a more awakened state from as early as during or just post world war 2. The more awakened children who are now in their 60's and 70's were here to help lay down the foundations for change and this can been seen with the huge changes that occurred in the 1960's and 1970's. From the late 1960's to 1990's (dates are approximate) saw the birth of even more evolved children, often these children viewed the boxed, societal view differently and got frustrated by the way that they were educated, expected to conform and how their creativity was not encouraged, they came to earth to begin to challenge how things were done. Many of these children were diagnosed with conditions such as ADHD and rather than helping them to forge their own paths and to understand why they behaved the way they did doctors just pumped them full of medication instead. There are a number of key traits that these children displayed including high intelligence, empathy, and intuitiveness, they may also have been seen as odd or strange and outside of the social norm. Other traits include:

- Rebellious - Rules and regulations make them feel stifled, they want to go their own path and do not want to have to fit in
- Introverted - They can withdraw from the world not wanting to conform and deal with other people and the negativity in the world
- Creative - They can be highly creative and are often attracted to the arts, theatre etc
- Excellent memory
- They often prefer to live in an imaginative world of their creation because they struggle to cope with how the world works

- Display skills and abilities that are intuitive and not learnt, brought from past lives
- They struggle with balancing emotions and sometimes fall into addiction or suffer from mental illness
- They may have innate or developed psychic abilities

In adulthood these traits may soften but there may be overwhelming feelings of being different or separate from the rest of society and a discontentment about the way of the world. They may also be driven to change things and want to make the world a better place. (If you feel that this was or is you and want to research more then look up the various writers that discuss Indigo children and adults)

Some children born from 1990 to 2010 (dates are approximate) have been born even more evolved and rather than challenging the system like their predecessors their role was and is more to bring peace and love and to bring people together. They are sensitive and caring and have a love of nature, they have a healing way about them and are often drawn to crystals. They are peacemakers who bring a calming feeling with them, they are sensitive, they tend to love music and will form lasting relationships. They may well be spiritual naturally, rejecting mainstream religion, possibly drawn to meditation and will not worry much about the past and see joy in each present moment. (If you recognise these traits in you or your children you can research Crystal Children)

From 2010 to date (again dates approximate) there have also been children born who are even more evolved, their connection to other dimensional realities is very strong and if encouraged they can recall past lives. These children are not as easily affected by negativity and can bring a lot of joy to their home. They can also be fearless because they trust their true self and are not affected by societal conditioning. They tend to have lots of energy and are deeply creative, they may well be gender and sexually fluid as they fully recognise their soul balance of both masculine and feminine energy. They can seem as if they live in their own world and are very clear about what they do and do not want which can be seen as stubbornness. They are very loving and generous and just want to make other people happy, they have no need for material things preferring to give things away or are happy with company of family or friends. (If you feel this is you or your child research Rainbow children)

There are many people who if asked feel that they come from the stars but do not quite know how to put into words why they feel that way. They tend to feel that they are old even at a young physical age, they often feel homesick as if they are searching for a place they lost and cannot find and this can sometimes lead to deep loneliness and even depression. They often find educational systems and standard philosophy limiting and have high levels of IQ and emotional intelligence with an ability to see a much bigger picture of how things are and get perplexed at why other people cannot see what they see. They are very empathic and have a deep inner knowing about other people's life challenges. Often survivors of bullying and, or abuse who struggle with low self-esteem and not loving themselves. They have few friends and people know that they are different and often feel the odd one out in their own families and feel much more comfortable with animals. Drawn to metaphysics and anything paranormal they also have strong 'imaginations' and vivid dreams. They also feel that they have a mission in life and have a strong urge to help people and change how things are in the world. They will also awaken to their true selves faster than others and are the ones who are in the world to show others the way to finding their true selves too. The biggest challenge for these people are to overcome the feelings of being limited on the earth plane and the abuse they have suffered to fully come into their true selves through the act of self-love. (If you feel that this describes you the you can further research Starseeds)

Types of Healing you will Experience

Moving from subconscious to conscious as you heal is a significant process and a big part of the healing journey. All of the memories and pain that you have buried beneath walls of ego induced protection begin to break down. As you move the thoughts, emotions and feelings relating to those memories what you are left with is wisdom. The wisdom of your lesson from that experience and how you can use that as you move forward deeper into your true self and how you can use that wisdom to help yourself and others as you move forward.

Self-healing

To be truly healthy and dis-ease free you require the correct mind, body, and spirit balance. Creating this balance is what self-healing is about, it is inner work on self-management of thoughts and emotions, Kyle Davies in his book The Intelligent Body explains 'there is a complex connection between your deep unconscious beliefs, your environment, and your behaviour. The extent to which you are free to be who you really are, to experience and express yourself unleashed and unbridled and without the insidious shackles of past conditioning can have a massive positive impact on your biology, neurology, physiology and psychology.' What Davies describes is indeed what the self-healing journey of ascension is all about, it is clearing deep unconscious beliefs from current and past lives. It is

171

about connecting to one's true self to re-discover what the heart and spirit desires and then to make changes internally and then externally to create life situations that allow free expression in love with the core focus being to let go of fear and replace it with love.

Healing occurs naturally within everyone's body, the mind body knows how to do this (Chopra &Tanzi The Healing Self) however there is a collective conscious belief particularly in the western world that healing needs to be supported by external chemical interventions which detract from the mind, body, and spirit balance. Tony Neate in his book New Dimensions in Healing discusses the damaging effects of any form of drug taking on the mind, body, and spirit balance, outlining that the chemicals interfere with the balance and prevent the spirit from doing what it does naturally and that is to heal. Chopra & Tanzi also discuss how the influence of mental attitude, emotions and will power can often be the difference in healing between one patient and another when using traditional medical intervention. A patient that may seem to have a worse illness can be cured if they have a more positive, determined belief that they can heal than a patient that doesn't and indeed suggest that it is this attitude and outlook that enables the body to heal and that then medical and chemical intervention is secondary.

The metaphysical self-healing practices recommended in this book can support the process of self-healing, indeed using a combination of practices to help to self-heal the mind, body, and spirit and bring about balance is good practice. Allow yourself to be intuitively led to a particular practice, to what is required or needed at the time and use self-awareness and 'listening' to the body (Pillars 1, 2 & 3) to help you make the right choices of practices and their effectiveness. The range and scope of metaphysical self-healing practices is wide and so is the application of some of them, so in order to consciously self-heal individuals need to be working towards a mind, body, and spirit balance and undertaking practices that support all areas. The physical body for example cannot be ignored in favour of just spiritual practices .

Self-healing is about an internal shift in energy, shifting the energy of past hurt, past emotions, being mindful of thoughts and corresponding emotions that can manifest into physical ailments. Louise Hay in You Can Heal Your Life discusses this and maintains that it is a conscious choice to be well and healthy. Making this choice for yourself and doing the activities, exercises and mediations in this book will initiate you into your journey of self-discovery and towards a healthier and happier life.

There are a number of types of healing that you will experience on your awakening journey, as discussed previously this will be self-healing but it is good to recognise and understand where this healing comes from. It is also important to allow the learning that comes from traumatic experiences to settle with you and become a part of your new conscious being.

Your true self is clever, it will guide you and take you through the stages of healing that are best for you, and will not expect your conscious self to endure anything that it cannot handle.

Healing Trauma

When many people think about trauma they often disregard themselves thinking that trauma is something serious that other people have experienced but that is not the case, I firmly believe that everyone has suffered trauma. What everyone in the world experienced with the Covid pandemic is trauma to the soul, being told what to do, where you can go and who you can see is an infringement of your divine rights as a human being and so it is trauma. The first thing that you have to do is to recognise that you have been through trauma and that it has caused pain to your mind, body, and spirit balance. Many people ignore the pain, bury the trauma and this can have catastrophic implications for the mind, body, and spirit. If you have experienced severe trauma then I advice you to seek out professional counselling to support you in healing.

The trauma that comes up for you may come across as a 'dream' or you may suddenly feel emotional and wonder why, you may even begin crying for no apparent reason. It is important that you go into yourself and identify where the pain is coming from. It could be inner child trauma, or from a particular event in your life or a series of events that link together. Searching out the cause of your pain is important for you to be able to let go of it and heal and it may take a while to do this as a lot of trauma has many layers that intertwine with other experiences in your life. Be kind and gentle to yourself during these times, self-care is vital. Journal about your experiences, talk to your trusted friend or mentor and cherish yourself in every way. Once you have identified the cause of your pain then it is good to ask yourself what it is that you learnt from the situation that caused the pain and from what it did to you when you buried it deep down within you. Self-forgiveness is so important and not judging the way dealt with the trauma also vital. Search for the key lessons that come from this enquiry as this supports the process of bringing knowledge from your subconscious to your conscious mind. This integration brings forth wisdom that allows you a much deeper understanding of yourself and others and enables you to respond rather than react. It enables you to love what was not loved before, it brings you deeper into you true self and to the happiness and joy you so deserve.

Shame is also a common emotion that is experienced by many who have experienced trauma. It is common to blame oneself for things that have happened. Shame can also come from things that one has done, things that are buried deep down, things that you may not have not told anyone else about, self-forgiveness and the recognition of the learning that you received from what happened is the way to heal from the feelings of shame.

Past Life Healing

As you go further into your awakening journey you will find that you may get dreams or visions in meditation of other places, people that you do not recognise, images of things that you do not remember happening to you in this lifetime and these will most likely be from a past or parallel lifetime. This information will be coming to you for a reason, firstly it teaches that you are more than the physical self, it teaches that who you are today is more than simply the experiences of this lifetime and it teaches that you are indeed consciousness having a human experience rather than a human body that has a spirit. What is also common is that there have been similar life themes across a number of lifetimes where wounding has occurred not only in this life but in others as well. Your true self will show them to you if they need to be healed alongside the trauma from this lifetime. There are layers to the healing process and there are often connections between past and parallel lives and your current incarnation. Allow your true self to guide you with making these connections and how you need to heal and let them go.

Seeing past lives also brings a different type of healing. It shows you how you have experienced different places, people and careers etc as a part of your spirits eternal development. This helps you to see and feel more connected to your true self and brings a greater sense of harmony and balance and peace that only internal knowing can bring. If you wish to explore past lives more, finding a reputable practitioner in past life regression to help guide you would be an excellent idea.

Metaphysical Causes of Illness

It is the culture of much of our society that when we get a physical pain or something wrong with our body we take medication or even a natural form of healing modality however finding the root cause of the problem is the only way that you will be rid of it permanently. As you develop your intuition you will find that you will instinctively know what the root cause of the physical or emotional symptoms are however you may find it useful to use a guide of suggestions as to the metaphysical causes of physical symptoms. Louise Hay, a pioneer in metaphysical teachings in her book Heal Your Body and in later editions of You Can Heal Your Life wrote a list of problems, probable causes and a positive affirmation to help change the thought pattern. This tool may help you with the identification of the issue you are experiencing. Often in the healing process we need a number of different methods or modalities to help us to heal fully. Many of the tools in this book will be a part of that in addition to the signposting that I have done to external practitioners and methods. The most important thing to remember is that each journey is unique and requires a unique way of healing. Please choose your WAY using guidance from your true self and always use the 7 Pillars of Personal Change to evaluate the effectiveness of any methods that you are using. Additionally if you choose to work with a practitioner, again use your intuition when searching for and choosing that person.

Ancestral Healing

Ancestral healing is used to clear generational pattens of behaviour, beliefs, intentions, and sacrifices that your ancestors made, created, experienced and so on.

Why might ancestral healing be relevant for you?

We are all aware that we carry the DNA of our parents, grandparents and other family members, it shows up in the colour of our eyes, skin, hair and so on but what is not so commonly known is that we also carry the genetic DNA, cell memory and energetic imprint of trauma, beliefs, patterns etc of our ancestors as well.

The imprint may manifest in a number of ways often subtle in nature, for example we may have an unexplained fear or phobia, you may feel things that somehow do not seem to belong to you, you may have patterns of behaviour that do not link with the rest of your life both current and past. It may be something more obvious that you see that you are repeating a pattern of a parent or grandparent. If an ancestor experienced war, died young, was murdered, had serious illness, had an addiction or other serious events, then the cell memory and energetic imprint of these experiences may be affecting your life currently. Another thing that can happen is that a phobia, pattern or belief may suddenly appear at a certain age, so for example your grandfather was shot in the back during WW2 when he was 32 and then you suddenly start feeling sharp pains in your back at the same age, this can be ancestral trauma affecting you, this can also happen from trauma that occurred in past lives too.

One way of identifying patterns is to make a family tree go back maybe 3 generations if you can and then next to each name write down any trauma or significant event that you are aware of that happened to them, then add to that a list of things that really defined who they were, their job or religion and so on. You could then work with a metaphysical practitioner who specialises in ancestral healing or a psychic medium or may be able to contact relatives that have passed over to assist in the healing of family trauma.

If you feel confident enough, you could start to clear ancestral patterns by doing some of the following things:

Stage 1

- Using the family tree, conversations with family and perhaps information from a medium to identify the patterns that exist that are ancestrally based
- Using the challenging beliefs exercise to identify the belief and track it to a particular ancestor
- Using Pillar 3 of The 7 Pillars of Personal Change to explore the intention and impact of the belief
- Fully recognise and acknowledge any sacrifices that were made by your ancestors

Stage 2

- Go into a meditative state and invoke your true self, guides, angels and your ancestors and ask them for permission to work on a shared trauma
- If you are not sure which ancestor you are carrying the ancestral trauma for, ask them to step forward and identify themselves
- Thank them and honour them for the pain they suffered and sacrifices they made
- Visualise the light of God Consciousness (consciousness of whomever you call God) healing all of the trauma

- Use the cord cutting exercise (on pages 180-181) to cut the cords with all of the trauma, invoke Arch Angel Michael to support you
- Using Pillars 4 - 7 identify new patterns of behaviour that will replace the old ancestral ones

Water Ceremony

Additionally you may want to do a water cleanse of your cell memory, water carries memory itself and can be really helpful in cleansing energetic imprints as well as physical ones.

Use the following ceremonial guidelines:

- Bring a jug of water and a glass, light a candle and settle into a light meditative state
- Invoke your true self, guides and angels
- Bless the water and say the following prayer over the water:

Blessed water flow deeply into every cell in my body and wash away the physical and energetic imprints of my ancestral trauma (you could be specific here about what the trauma, pattern or belief is), purify my cells and send them my love

- Drink a glass of the water and then meditate deeply for 5 minutes then drink another glass and meditate again, during the meditation visualise the water going into every cell of your body and healing, then visualise the light of God Consciousness (consciousness of whomever you call God) going into each cell and healing

You can use this ceremony to support the healing of other forms of trauma as well.

Releasing Trauma Exercise

You can do this exercise as a part of the process of letting go of pain and trauma as a part of your healing journey:

Make a list of the trauma, issues, problems, pain that you experienced. Then go outside to a place that is special to you, this could be in your garden or somewhere where you walk or by water whatever feels right for you.

- Sit and go into a mediative state and call in your personal guides and angels and invoking your true self to be with you
- Visualise white light surrounding you
- Take 3 deep breaths and begin reading your list, as you go through the pain or traumatic events or hurts experienced breathe into the emotions that come up for you and as you feel the emotions breathe them out of your body
- Once you have completed reading the list and breathing out the emotions, take your list and burn it asking that the pain, hurt and trauma be ignited into the flames of divine love
- Be grateful for the release
- Go and do some self-care activity to take care of your mind, body, and spirit

Metaphysical Cord Cutting

There is another exercise that can really help with the healing of wounding and trauma and that is metaphysical cord cutting. Whether it is with people, places or situations and events there are energetic cords that connect from your energetic body (or aura) to that person, place or event. The cords allow for energy exchange between the two things and this means that the emotions, thoughts, and feelings connected to them can continue to affect you. As humans we use the mechanism of crying to release pain and this is very healing, adding cord cutting to that can help to fully heal the wound or to stop the energetic influence of another person. Using the following cord cutting exercise and prayer will help you to do this:

Sit somewhere quiet where you can bring yourself into a light meditative state by focusing on deep breathing and relaxing the body. Once you feel calm and peaceful, call in Arch Angel Michael to help you oversee the cord cutting and then visualise the person, situation or event (or all 3 if needed), then visualise the energetic cords that go between you and that person or event.There may be several cords, visualise them all, allow them to come into focus in your mind's eye. Say the following prayer:

I release (name of person or situation or both) with love, I accept and am grateful for the lessons I learned. I take back all the energy that has been taken from me or that I gave away and return any energy that I took. I free myself (and anyone else involved) from all ties that bind us and I cut the cords and dissolve them into the light. I send all energy back to where it came from with love, peace and forgiveness. And so it is.

You can now visualise a large pair of scissors cutting the cords and then see the cords break and dissolve into bright white light. Thank Arch Angel Micheal for his assistance.

Decluttering

Making room in your home for a new way of being is really important so that the energy can flow and the environment that you live in is more conducive to your awakening journey. It is very common for us to build up material things around us that represent past memories, people we have loved and lost, childhood items, inherited things from grandparents and parents and so on. Many people also find that they buy items that they don't really need because the process of shopping gives them a sense of temporary fulfilment.

Decluttering your home can start with your wardrobe, how many items of clothing do you own that you do not wear or have not worn for some time? Take the opportunity to spend some time having a clear out! Then go through the rest of you home and donate to charity or clear out items that you no longer want or need. The less material things you have cluttering up your living space the more the energy will flow through your home and support your awakening journey.

You also need to have some personal space where you can be alone, to meditate, to journal and work through the thoughts, feelings and emotions that your awakening journey will create. This may be a challenge if you live with a partner and children but try to find somewhere. Even if you have a spot in a garden or balcony that you can spend time alone. Make sure you set boundaries with the people you live with too, so when you want alone time they know not to disturb you.

Nature & Animals

The importance of nature and pets should not be underestimated. There is a deep synergy between Mother Earth and the humans on this planet and for too long that connection and need for balance has been ignored by the majority. Spending time in nature whether it be walking, hiking, sitting by a tree, swimming in the ocean, and interacting with animals is all beneficial to humans. The pure loving energy that we get from Mother Earth heals our mind, body, and spirit and contributes to the balance that we need to achieve in our lives. Spending regular time in nature is really important for us all. It gives us the space to heal, the time to allow us to be with ourselves and the beautiful earth, to find our place amongst the beauty and see the beauty reflecting back to us and within us. When we look deeply at nature and the creatures in the world we can learn much from them, each flower, tree and animal can teach us something about life and ourselves. It also helps us to learn how we affect the earth in the way that we live, the things that we do and can help us see how we can make changes in the way that we do things to create more of a balance between ourselves and the earth. I urge you to spend more time reconnecting yourself to the natural world around you and to reflect on the part in which you play in creating a better balance between how you live and impact the earth. This balance brings you more synergistically in alignment with the world that you are a part of and supports you in your awakening and healing journey. I would go as far as to say that spending time in nature regularly is an essential part of your journey and your life.

Pets

The animals that we choose to bring into our homes are in many cases incredibly loved and cherished but the amount of cruelty and abuse of animals that still goes on in the world is extremely saddening. I am going to predominately talk about cats and dogs as the most common pets in this next section however the principles I outline can be applied to any animal.

Animals are very connected to both the earth dimension and the higher realms and I am sure if you have ever owned a dog or a cat you have seen them at one time or another looking at or following something that you could not see. Pets are here to teach us about unconditional love. No matter how bad a day you have had, how you look or feel, they love you anyway. They are there to greet you when you come home, when you pick them up or hug them you feel better because they give you unconditional love, it really is the most beautiful gift! Often animals of the same breed can have similarities in their behaviour but all of them have their own individual personalities. Pets are also very sensitive to energy and to mood, body language and tone of voice. We use tone commonly when discipline is needed to prevent damage to the home for example. It goes beyond that though, the environment that the animal lives in is mirrored in its behaviour back to its human companions. Give the pet a beautiful loving, positive environment with little negativity, no arguments, shouting or discord and it will be at its happiest. However if those things are regularly in play at the home in which the pet lives they are going to become anxious, nervous and the consequent behaviour could manifest in anything from being withdrawn and aloof to damaging furniture and attacking owners and other animals. Even if the prime owner (or leader of the pack as many dog breeds see their human prime owner) is in a constant state of stress can trigger poor behaviour in their pet. Anyone who has fostered or adopted a rescue pet will know how much effort it takes to undo old patterns of behaviour created by past abuse and will also know that the results can be extremely rewarding. In this way our pets teach us how we should behave towards other human beings, if we offered the same amount love, kindness, compassion and understanding firstly to ourselves and then to others our world would be in a much better state. Pets also communicate with us. Their ways are more subtle but taking the time to really listen to them and understand what they are trying to say to you not only helps them but can be very rewarding in your relationship with them.

Numbers

Numbers like anything else have an energy or vibration, when you look deeply at the universe you see that everything has a numerical signature underpinning it. In nature, in the cosmos, in our everyday lives numbers are given significance from the date, our birth to the use of numbers that are seen as lucky (7), or unlucky (13). Numbers can also be used to help unlock your life purpose, they are used in the tarot for example. As you awaken you will notice that you see sequences of numbers more often for example 11:11 or 2.22 and so on. Metaphysically these numbers indicate messages or synchronicities that may be coming from your true self, your guides or angels or to confirm that something you feel or think is accurate. Take note of what you were thinking or feeling when you see these sequences of numbers or something that you were talking about. You will find that there is a link between the numbers you see and what you were thinking, feeling or talking about.

The vibration of the different numbers and their meaning can be researched. There are different explanations for the numbers so find one that resonates for you and then you can use numerology to help you support your awakening and in the projects that are important to you in your life. You may feel drawn to a particular number or feel that a sequence of numbers fit right for you. You may even want to use those numbers in phone numbers, when choosing an address to live at or in your business or work. Do what feels right for you, experiment and have fun with numbers!

Astrological Impacts

Most people are aware that the moon cycles affects humans every month but you may not have been aware of the impact of astrological events and the planets on the human energetic body and on human lives. You may have read your stars and wondered how the astrologists reached their predictions and may even have thought that it was a lot of nonsense!

It is not until you realise how the planets affect the earth's magnetic field and in turn our own energetic body that you begin to get more of an understanding as to how and why we do indeed get affected by cosmic events. We know from my description earlier in the book that we send, receive and process energy through our chakras. The energy that we receive comes from various sources including other humans, animals, and other electromagnetic fields including the earth's geomagnetic field. Some of the energy we receive is not good for us, from some human made electric magnetic sources for example and this affects our energetic body and in turn our physical, emotional, mental and spiritual bodies (the layers of our auric body). Mother Earth herself emanates energy both within the atmosphere and outwards into the cosmos, and her magnetic field is affected by other planets and stars in our galaxy because each of them emit magnetic patterns that are transmitted to earth via the solar winds. Each of the planets also create gravitational fluctuations within the magnetosphere that surrounds the earth. Any changes to the earths magnetic fields stimulates humans' nervous systems thus affecting all four levels, physical, emotional, mental and spiritual. According to Pamela Welch in her book The Energy Body Connection when she discusses archetypal themes of the different planets giving examples such as Jupiter representing the teacher archetype and Venus the artist archetype, she explains that each planet has an archetype and they consist of a range of attributes such as Mars the warrior and Venus the lover, the lists for each planet are quite complex. These planetary archetypes were first drawn out by the Ancient Greek astrologers when the planets, the sun and moon were called Gods and Goddesses, the attributes assigned to each planet have since been analysed by looking at the alignment and movement of each planet and the resulting affect on human life both collectively and individually and the work of the Ancient Greeks holds up well in modern times.

Astrology and our Birth

The planets, sun, moon and stars are constantly moving and as such are in different alignments at different times. The particular alignment of the cosmos at the time of our birth sets a mark on our nervous and energetic systems and sets the theme for our lives that is directly connected to the archetypes of the cosmic alignment in place at the time of our birth. We plan in alignment with our life plan that we agree before we incarnate and so the particular planetary configuration at our birth actually supports our chosen life path. The planets closest to earth have much faster impacts on our lives whilst the planets further away are classed as slow planets and the impacts are more gradual and last longer, influencing more of our major life changes.

Impact on our Lives

The impact of cosmic configuration on our lives will affect us in different ways. If we are not on our chosen life path, say in a career that is not in alignment with our life purpose then this causes conflict within and affects our four bodies (physical, emotional, mental and spiritual) and our whole energetic system. This lack of alignment contributes to our being more in our outward persona rather than our true self. Then when the cosmic forces affect us and trigger what our true self and our true life path is supposed to be it creates conflict within.

Astrological Alignment & Awakening

The global awakening that I discussed at the beginning of the book is happening now because of the unique alignment of the planets. The end of the Age of Pisces and the transition into the Age of Aquarius, cosmic alignment, and energy coming from that alignment support the awakening. Additionally traits of the planetary influences are right and in position for supporting the awakening of humanity.

People who have not started their awakening journey are often not aware of the impact of cosmic alignment on their lives but as you awaken and begin your journey to your true self you will find that you become much more aware. The more you are aligned with your true self and on your correct life path the easier the impact of the planets will be.

A further example of planetary alignment is in August in the constellation of Leo, there is an alignment with the star Sirius on and around August 8th which is called Lion's Gate, the star comes into alignment with the pyramid in Giza and in the sky it appears to be closer to earth. Cosmic energy is most powerful between Sirius and Earth at this time and so makes it a perfect opportunity to meditate and connect with this energy as it supports the embodiment of the true self.

Astrological Alignment & Healing

As a part of the unique astrological alignment that we are currently experiencing, together with your awakening journey and a higher sensitivity to cosmic events you will find that healing cosmic energy begins to support and guide your healing journey. Guided by your true self who will take opportunities in alignment with cosmic placement to bring about healing of issues relating to trauma, inner child wounding, past life healing and physical healing at a pace that it feels your physical, emotional, mental and physical self can cope with. You will notice that as certain cosmic events occur such as full and new moons, retrogrades, planets and stars in particular constellations, you will experience strong emotions, remembering of past events, issues in your life that are a part of the healing that is needed on your journey to your true self. During these times it is important to use Pillars 1-3 particularly, so that you are aware of what is coming through you and can allow the healing to occur and let the pain go.

Moon Influences

The moon influences earth's oceans tides and indeed the water in our bodies. Metaphysically the moon represents our inner world and the feminine within whilst the sun represents our masculine self and our outer world. The cycles of the moon remind us of the cycles in our lives, the beginnings and the endings and can bring great comfort and flow to life. We tend to sleep less at full moon and are more likely to have vivid dreams that are sending messages about our lives (or the influence of past lives on our current life). Many ancient and indigenous cultures believe that women menstruate at new moon and when they are in sync with the moon phases they are more able to harness their feminine creative power.

During the lunar cycles, particularly at new and full moon when energies are strongest, there is a large influence on our emotions, our emotional storehouse based on past experiences, and our subconsciously hidden fears, anxieties and worries. During these times you may find that you are particularly sensitive and need to be aware of what is coming from the subconscious to the conscious mind so that you can work through how you feel and do a lot of self-care. Although some of the healing can be painful, the release that comes as a result of the healing can feel really good. It also makes way for more positivity and more of your true self to emerge in everyday life.

At new moon it can also be a good time to clear away old patterns, do the decluttering, conduct clearing meditations or healing practices and to set intentions or positive affirmations for the month ahead.

At full moon is the time when emotions are at their highest and it is good to reflect on what you have achieved during the last lunar cycle and to be really aware of any strong emotions, irritations, friction, and actively manage how you feel and flow your emotions through you. Part of that management could be to meditate in the light of the full moon and ask the energy to support you in releasing all that you wish to at that time.

Getting in Rhythm with Nature

When we look at how natural life on earth is perfectly designed and flows with the elements and with the earth's position around the sun and within the galaxy you begin to realise that humans are meant to also be in rhythm with nature too. No matter where you live in the world you are influenced by nature, in areas that are away from the poles or the equator there are seasons that are in line with how close a particular part of the world is to the sun. These seasons influence how we live but in the modern world we try our best to circumnavigate around this and carry on our lives in a similar way all year round. Our physical bodies particularly are affected by the flow of nature, the changing seasons, the energy of the changing times, the flow of birth through growth to death and so on affect us. Think about how emotionally you feel better on a sunny day or rainy day if you like that, we are influenced by the weather a lot! Attuning ourselves to the flow of the seasons and using the different shift points throughout the year to support what we are doing in our lives will allow the energy of our lives to flow more easily, equinoxes and solstices are good examples. In spring everything is new and comes to life and grows, the spring equinox is a perfect time when the light of the sun and the dark of night are equal (12 hours of each), to bring forth new things into your life to connect deeply with the earth and the universe and to your true self, you can also let go of the things that do not serve you and your life purpose. Summer is when everything flourishes and new life is growing, the summer solstice which is the longest day of light is a time to reaffirm your connection with your own light and that of everyone else, to harness the energy of the sun to help you move your life, dreams, and purpose and give them a boost. During autumn we see the harvest of the fruits of our labour and when it comes to the autumn equinox it is a time for us to reflect upon how well we did that year and to be grateful for all that we have. Winter is a time for rest, recuperation and to plan the year ahead, the winter solstice on the shortest day of light in the year is a chance to let go of old patterns and habits, and to renew and reflect.

Meditating on the equinoxes and solstices and focussing on the significance of each event gives you an opportunity to be supported by the energy and consciousness around you, I highly recommend it!

Being in rhythm with nature also means eating naturally, using natural medicines, using natural and holistic therapies, spending time in nature to allow the beauty of nature to support you on your journey of life. You will find that the more you align with the rhythm of nature the more easily your life will flow. It will also be much easier for you to connect to, and be with, your true self, enabling you to create the life that you want and deserve.

Unity

As you go along your awakening journey you start to step away from just thinking and feeling things purely about the self and the people directly in your life to thinking more about others and how you can help the people around you. We often see great unity when there is a tragedy or a crisis when people truly pull together and help one another. The shock, trauma and empathy goes deeply into the heart and this is what moves people into action and unity. After the initial events fade so does that sense of unity in most cases and people go back to being selfish and self-centred about their own world.

Awakening changes that, once you have worked on yourself and moved forward you will find more and more that you have a desire to help others, to pass on your knowledge and do things to support your community. This can be in many different ways and does not have to involve getting stuck into big projects with others but could be as simple as recommending a book that helped you or having a coffee and listening to a friend and making the chat about them. Even smiling at strangers in the street and being happy around people, asking the shop assistant if they are having a good day, opening a door for someone, small things that have a big impact on others are the truly beautiful things that can make another persons day.

Moving forward, unity will be an important part of how our society will operate, working together in ways that we have never done before to ensure that EVERYONE has opportunity, is looked after, educated and has all they need on a daily basis. You can start to be a part of that by doing your bit, start with smiling, and then move onto the small things. Who knows where that will lead you, perhaps to bigger and greater things and for you to be a real part of the change that is need in our communities and society as a whole. Ultimately we are all one human race and we have a responsibility to each other to take care and look out for one another.

If you feel drawn to wanting to do more to build a new and better community check out the United People Foundation: www.unitedpeople-foundation.org

Working towards Self-Love

All of the teachings in this book have been guiding you towards developing self-love, recognising and taking into your heart the truth that you are a beautiful divine being that deserves the best of everything that this physical life has to offer, this is the journey of self-love. Self-love is the gift that you are going to give yourself on this beautiful awakening journey, and remember that it is a journey and not a destination. There are layers upon layers of self-love and the further you go on your journey the deeper you will go and more layers that you will heal and peel away to take you closer and closer to being your true self all the time. Your true self will guide you on this journey and your job is to listen, allow and act on this guidance and to recognise when your ego or your wounded inner child is in control and how they may be blocking your path to self-love. Noticing the subtle changes that you make in this self-love journey, how you feel, behave, think, and are, and when shifts and changes happen within you is also important. It shows you that you are progressing and achieving your goals. Giving yourself rewards when you have achieved a goal or passed a milestone is also a really good way of supporting your self-love journey. Using the 7 Pillars of Personal Change as a way of life will also support you, the cyclical nature of the model helps you be mindfully aware of how you are doing on your journey and what you need to do next.

Semiotic Writing of an Awakening Experience - Tapestry

Based on the writings of a beloved friend

An ancient tapestry that has many layers, with lots of dark colours, when you look at the tapestry in a certain way you catch fleeting fragments of an iridescent rainbow buried deeply in the weaving. One single thread comes loose and a cat latches onto that thread, and the unravelling begins. As the tapestry begins to unravel, the story begins to change like moving stairs that continually alter your direction. The dark colours that are filled with pain and suffering start to lose their strength, their darkness, and their power. As you stare at the tapestry in a pure light, the shimmering rainbow is longing to be set free, as the dark tapestry is unravelling, another one has begun, beneath. This tapestry is elusive, hidden beneath the dark colours of pain but the rainbow colours of your true self, the original tapestry that you are begins to weave colours of joy, peace, love, wisdom, trust and magick. Multiple layers of your ancient stories filled with pain and sadness begin to dissolve and the tapestry beneath comes alive. Listen and hear a melodic beating in a rhythm that hums the colours of the rainbow, feel the vibration of the colours as you are reborn. The iridescence of the rainbow colours is even more brilliant than the original threads of your life. The rainbow colours of your true self begin creating an astounding tapestry weaving breathtaking colourful threads that will create a legacy of unconditional love. You cannot see the rainbow tapestry yet but you can feel it being woven together, you hear the rhythm, the hum of your heart that beats within the universe as one.

Final Note

An awakening journey is one of discovery and healing and is cyclical and after each cycle you progress onto the next level. Being guided by your intuition is vital through these cycles to help you to navigate the roller coaster ride of emotions that you will experience. You need to be brave but the rewards are great. Each cycle brings more light, more love, more trust, more wisdom and more joy, I wish all of these things for you now and always.

Namaste

Merlin

Final Prayer

I channelled the following prayer as a version of Psalm 23, for me this depicts the true meaning of the Psalm and my greatest wish is for you is to take the words of the prayer into your heart and make it your own.

I am my own Shepherd, I am fully abundant

My higher self guides me to rest in the heart of Mother Earth and encourages me to drink from the pure waters of her compassionate love

My higher self gives me strength and guides me in every aspect of my life

Even through the darkest times of my life I will never feel fear, for God resides within me

The light of my divine soul wields my own sword of truth, personal power, and pure heart

When I stand in any dark energy the light of my divinity shines so brightly that it cancels out the darkness

I know that abundance and love with be with me all the days of my life because God lives within me for eternity

REFERENCE LIST

www.anandawellness.com

www.ons.gov.uk

www.relaxmodalities.com

Sheri Jacobson @ www.harleytherapy.co.uk

TheHolisticTherapist

www.nhs.uk

www.thebowentechnique.com

www.smarthealing.com.au

Tolle, Echart, The Power of Now. 2005 3rd Edition Hodder and Stoughton U.K.

Brennan, Barbara Ann, Hands of Light. 1987 Bantam Books U.S.A.

Brennan, Barbara Ann, Light Emerging. 1993 Bantam Books U.S.A.

Chopra, Deepak, & Tanzi, Rudolph E. The Healing Self. Penguin. Print 2018

Davies, Kyle. The Intelligent Body. WW Norton & Company. Print 2017

Hay, Louise, You can heal your Life. Hay House UK 2005

Neate, Tony. New Dimensions in Healing. Eye of Gaza Press. Print 2007

Tammekand, Ronald, Symptoms of Spiritual Awakening 2020

Eason, Cassandra, The New Crystal Bible. Carlton Books 2010

Ashby, Nina, Colour Therapy, Plain and Simple. Hampton Roads Publishing company U.S.A 2018

Oxford English Dictionary

Chia, Mantak with Winn, Michael, Taoist Secrets of Love, Cultivating Male Sexual Energy. Aurora Press, U.S.A. 1984

Welch, Pamela, The Energy Body Connection. Llewellyn Publications, U.S.A. 2000

CPSIA information can be obtained
at www.ICGtesting.com
Printed in the USA
BVHW071241210621
610124BV00002B/221